Real People Don't Own Monkeys

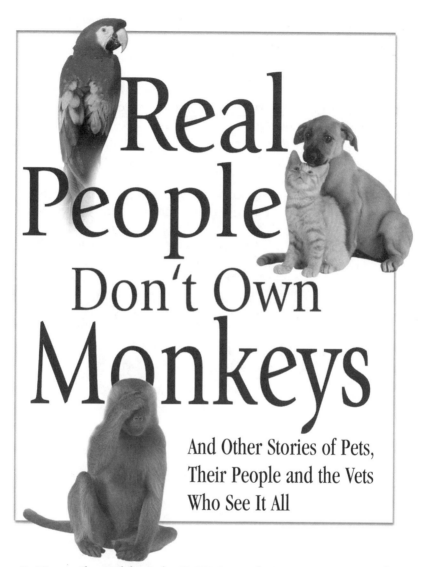

Real People Don't Own Monkeys

And Other Stories of Pets,
Their People and the Vets
Who See It All

J. Veronika Kiklevich, D.V.M., with Steven N. Austad

SOURCEBOOKS, INC.
NAPERVILLE, ILLINOIS

Published by Sourcebooks, Inc.
P.O. Box 4410, Naperville, Illinois 60567-4410
(630) 961-3900
FAX: (630) 961-2168
www.sourcebooks.com

Library of Congress Cataloging-in-Publication Data

Printed and bound in the United States of America
VP 10 9 8 7 6 5 4 3 2 1

For Helen, who always believed in me

Contents

Preface

My life has revolved around pets. As a child, my pets were any and all animals that I could manage to catch and drag into the house. With two daughters now, I am even more appreciative than I used to be of the tolerance my mother Helen had for my animal obsession. She even encouraged it.

I knew that I wanted to be a veterinarian since the age of three, when my mother informed me that I couldn't grow up to be a horse. At eleven, I began working in a veterinary hospital after school and on weekends, and I continued working in various hospitals throughout high school and college, until I went away to vet college at Cornell.

Because I have always loved animals of all kinds, I assumed from the first that I would have a "mixed" veterinary practice, one that treated not only dogs and cats, but large farm animals too. It didn't work out that way. In vet school, I discovered that my absence of fear around animals was not compatible with working around species large enough to kill you by accident. After being kicked, stomped, and squashed within a few inches of my life several times, I decided I should stick to animals small enough that if they killed me, it would have to be on purpose.

So professionally, I have concentrated on smaller animals, but I've had a mixed practice anyway—a mixture of traditional pets and those known in the trade as exotics. My general rule is that if you can get it into my exam room, I will examine and treat it as best I can. So besides all the standard breeds of dogs and cats, I've examined birds from the size of wrens to the size of emus. I've treated monkeys, snakes, iguanas, ferrets, rabbits, squirrels, raccoons, rats, mice, tarantulas, guinea pigs, pot-bellied pigs, goats, and just about anything else you can imagine. I've never minded if a particular pet was fierce, and I've got the scars to prove it. In fact, people who see my bare arms outside working hours must wonder what I do for a living. Professional sword fighter or knife sharpener, perhaps?

My husband, Steve, also has spent his life with animals. Now an academic zoologist, he formerly trained large wild animals (lions, tigers, bears, elephants) for the Hollywood movie business. In the course of that work, he also dealt with the exotic pet subculture, which could as easily be called the exotic people subculture. Someone might (indeed, someone did) phone him in the middle of the night to ask for help getting a pet tiger out from under her bed. Someone else would ask him if he could help find a well-behaved lion for his adolescent daughter's birthday present. Other people's problem pets, like monkeys or elephants that had bit the neighbor's children or gored an innocent passerby, were sometimes hidden at his animal compound until the heat died down.

We have worked together on any number of animals during his field research over the years. These studies of everything from birds to beetles to opossums, squirrels, and spiders have taken us to exotic locales on three continents. Whenever we spent significant time in the bush, I would always manage to find a pet. It might be Penny, the hen; Orejas, the pig; Pegajosa, the calf; or a baby bird that had fallen out of its nest. Sometimes these pets were healthy. But more often, seeing a sick or injured animal aroused my veterinary instincts, and I would soon adopt it.

Not surprisingly, the pets we have had in our own home over the years would make a pretty decent zoo by themselves. Right now, for instance, we have a guinea pig, a squirrel, an iguana, various other lizards, a turtle, a hedgehog, several kinds of parrots, and the usual assortment of dogs and cats. Well, not exactly the usual assortment. Our terrier has three legs, and our dachshund has a heart pacemaker. We released the coyote and the raccoons once they were healthy. The python died, the cockatoo we gave away...you get the idea.

We have learned a great deal from our experiences with animals—about the animals themselves and about the people who own them. Certain pets require a certain sort of owner. Take monkeys, for instance.

The trouble with monkeys is that they bite. Invariably. It's not a matter of whether, it's only who and when. Actually, that's only one of the troubles with monkeys. Another is that they will fling their feces at you when they get upset. If you give them a chance, they will also rip your earrings off your ears, break your glasses, maybe poke out an eye. Monkeys will win no olfactory prizes, either. They usually smell like they've been playing in a sack of dead rabbits.

The trouble with monkey owners is that they find these traits simply adorable. So most veterinarians would rather examine a spitting cobra than a monkey. But I enjoy the challenge. With monkeys, the main challenge a vet faces is how to restrain them so you can perform a proper examination without being bitten, and without the owner thinking you are mistreating their little cutie. It was gratifying to figure that out. Later on, I'll let you in on the secret of how to hold a monkey as easily as if it had a handle.

I enjoy the color and quirks of the owners as much as those of the animals. These owners and I are two of a kind, really. Animal enthusiasts—fanatics. They just don't have a smock and a profession to cover for them like I do.

During my medical career, I've been fortunate enough to host a radio call-in program and a television show. As I developed my on-air persona, I almost subconsciously developed the habit of illustrating various veterinary problems and procedures by telling stories about my own, or my husband's, experiences with pets and their owners. People seemed to enjoy and remember these tales, sometimes more than the specific advice I gave them. So he and I finally decided to write down a few of these adventures, in the hopes that other people might find them as instructive and amusing as we had.

Here is a sampling of our experiences. To my clients, colleagues, and former students who discover themselves pseudonymously present here, please don't take offense.

Try to feel flattered. I've focused on my own foibles more than anyone else's. We all have our ridiculous moments. We all make mistakes. If other people can get a laugh when we make fools of ourselves, and if we can learn from our mistakes, then the world is indeed a wonderful place.

I've included a fair amount of practical advice about various sorts of pets along the way. With luck, that advice may save you a few dollars and some grief in dealing with your own animals. What else might the stories do for you? Well, laughter is supposedly therapeutic. Maybe they will save you at least one trip to the shrink.

Introduction

The collie seems to be bleeding to death. My guess is that it's cancer—most likely a ruptured hemangiosarcoma, cancer of the blood vessels. Not good news. "Let's wrap it, start a transfusion, get a CT ASAP." I leave my intern, Scott, to take care of these things. Unlike some of my interns, he has turned out to be capable, energetic, and even better, he knows what he knows and admits what he doesn't know. I can be sure he'll ask me for help if he needs it.

A message on my pager informs me that a limping Labrador with a large lump on its back is in Room 2, and a cat with possible antifreeze poisoning has just been carried through the front door. I send Katie, a shy, pretty student who looks about fourteen years old, to take a history on the Labrador and record its temperature, pulse, and respiration rate. Katie is not a big help yet. She lacks confidence and her knowledge of physiology could be better. Also, she is still in a snit because I yelled at her yesterday for miscalculating an anesthesia dose. What if she'd actually given that dose? We'd have a dead cat and possibly a lawsuit on our hands, and I'd be depressed all weekend.

My pager screeches again. "Mrs. Donegan is on the phone, she wants..." I turn off the pager. I know what

Mrs. Donegan wants. It can wait. Right now, I need to see if there is any hope for the poisoned cat. The two HBC's (hit-by-cars) that were admitted last night don't seem to be quite so urgent. They are resting quietly in the intensive care unit. One has two broken legs for sure, and possibly a ruptured bladder. The other one is a neuro case. It was having seizures for most of the night, but is quiet now. No one has been able to locate either of the owners. My technician has discovered that Dr. Bagley, the neurologist, is back from his meeting and will be in within the next hour. He can look at the neuro case. I should probably examine the fracture and decide whether to refer it straight to orthopedics or do something about the bladder. No, Sara, my new technician can examine the bladder and get back to me. Thank God I have Sara. My previous technician wouldn't have known a bladder from a Brazil nut. I'd better get to that poisoned cat first. It's too bad that those nice people with the parrot, who have already waited patiently for nearly an hour, will have to wait a bit longer. But their parrot will still be alive an hour from now. I'm not so sure about the cat.

They call me Dr. K. I've been Dr. K from the time I realized that not many people could pronounce Kiklevich without sounding like they were choking. Welcome to my life. If I don't have a couple of more balls in the air than I can comfortably juggle, something is wrong.

I am a clinical instructor at Washington State University Veterinary Teaching Hospital. This means that I run a walk-in animal clinic. A lot of times the animals don't walk in, they have to be carried. My job is to ensure that they can walk out. I do my best. I try to give my patients the highest quality of medical care available anywhere, and at the same time I teach senior veterinary students about the life they will lead after graduation. That is, the life of a real-life veterinary hospital, as opposed to the life of textbooks, tough exams, late nights, laboratory exercises, and demanding instructors they have now. As senior students, they should know the anatomy of the circulatory system in exquisite detail, but will they be able to hit a jugular vein with a hypodermic needle and calculate the right drug dose when an animal is seconds away from death if they fail? They should know all about the brain and a lot about animal behavior, but will they be able to comfort a grieving client who has just lost her best friend in the world? By the time they finish working with me, they will, or I hope they seek another line of work.

I haven't always worked at a teaching hospital. After graduating from Cornell, I went to work in a six-doctor private veterinary clinic in Albuquerque, New Mexico. Later on, when my husband got a job on the faculty at Harvard, I joined a smaller, but superb, pet hospital on Boston's South Shore. I've been fortunate in the doctors I've worked with. They've been intelligent, compassionate, willing to learn throughout their professional lives, and willing to let me continue learning too. They've also been committed to the finest medicine and surgery. I couldn't work under any other conditions. I interviewed at more than a dozen hospitals in the Boston area before I found one that shared my standards and philosophy.

The pace here may seem hectic. It is hectic. The students think they're stressed, but they don't know what real stress is yet. Wait until they kill their first animal because they were rushed and stupidly overconfident, or until an owner can't afford the treatment that would save her pet for sure. The students also don't yet appreciate how much we need a good laugh around this place. Humor keeps us sane. Fortunately, there is plenty of humor available if you just look around.

The students should appreciate the positive side of this job, the emotional rewards. Why else would they put themselves through the torture of vet school? There are few things in life as gratifying as saving an animal's life when everyone else was sure it would die, or watching a handful of squirming puppies you've just delivered by Cesarean section, or returning a purring elderly cat to a grateful elderly owner.

The poison case turns out not to be as bad as it might have been. The cat had swallowed antifreeze all right. They love that stuff. So do dogs. So do kids, for that matter. It tastes sweet. Why don't the manufacturers add something to antifreeze to make it foul-tasting to kids and animals? We must lose dozens of dogs and cats each year to antifreeze poisoning just in our hospital.

Fortunately, this cat hadn't swallowed a great deal of it, and it was not too long ago. Scott, having stabilized the bleeding collie and shipped it off to radiology, is now ready to take over. As I walk out the door, I tell him to explain to the students why he will be able to save this cat's life with an intravenous infusion of vodka. They think I'm joking. For once, I'm not. I'll explain how it works later. Katie tells me that she found bilateral shoulder pain in the Labrador. That was a good observation. She may make a good doctor yet.

Time now to have a look at the parrot. Yikes, the waiting room is full. At least it's quieter out here. "Hello, I'm Dr. K. Let's take…I bet her name is Polly…in the back and have a look at her." My student flock migrates with me to the examination room. The day seems to be shaping up just about like normal.

Microwave Cat

Honesty is not just the best policy, it is the only policy for a veterinarian—even if it might sometimes seem more compassionate to stretch the truth. I found this out the hard way early in my career from a cat named Twinkle.

Twinkle was one of those particularly tiny part-Siamese cats who never seem to quite grow up. As an adult, she was as sweet and cuddly as a kitten—even to me, the doctor who injected or impolitely inspected her every time we met. Twinkle's owner (whom I'll call Joyce) was a dream client. She trusted me completely. Whatever I decided was best for Twinkle's health was fine. Period. Money was no object.

Joyce brought Twinkle in to see me one morning because of what seemed to be a minor problem. For about a day, Twinkle hadn't been eating well, nor drinking much, and she was unusually lethargic. As usual, the physical exam didn't tell me much, so I drew some blood for testing and began giving her intravenous fluids and antibiotics. This is the basic veterinary shotgun approach, which we often use while we're trying to discover what's really wrong.

By afternoon, Twinkle looked somewhat better. Joyce, who had been worriedly phoning me every couple of hours to talk over Twinkle's condition, was relieved and so was I. However, Twinkle took a sudden, unexplained turn for the worse later that evening and went downhill fast. She died around midnight.

I'm not sure if I was more exhausted or depressed or just discouraged by then, but I knew for sure that I needed to be somewhere by myself for a few minutes. As I walked out the door to go weep quietly by myself, I told my new technician to "do something with the body," by which I meant wrap her in a blanket and set her aside until I spoke with Joyce in the morning. The technician assumed I meant put Twinkle in the freezer and that's just what she did.

For Twinkle, here is where the problem ended. For me, here is where the problem began. Probably the hardest thing a veterinarian has to do is tell people that their beloved pet has died unexpectedly. Even though we have to deal with grief all the time, there is something particularly wrenching about the grief of an unanticipated catastrophe. I thought this might get easier for me as my career progressed, but it hasn't. It remains to this day the most difficult thing I do. However at that time, the beginning of my career, I developed what seemed to me a humane way of handling these situations. I let owners down easy.

If an animal died unexpectedly, I would phone the owner and begin gradually preparing them for the bad news. "Poopsie's condition has worsened," I might say, "I'll keep an especially close eye on her and let you know if there's any change." A couple of hours later, I'd phone back. "Things are looking worse. I don't think there's much hope, but I'm trying everything I can." Several hours after that—by now quite a number of hours after the animal had actually died—I would finally force myself to break the news. "I'm calling with bad news. Poopsie died a few minutes ago." Then we would usually have a mutual weeping session over the phone.

This technique was easier for me, of course, than the immediate brutal truth. And I still think it may be a more humane way to break bad news to owners than the frank way I do it now. However in Twinkle's case, it was nearly a disaster. "Joyce," I said, phoning early the next morning, "Twinkle's condition has worsened. I'll keep an especially close eye on her and let you know if there's any change."

"Oh my God, I have to see her!" shrieked Joyce as she literally left the phone dangling and bolted out the door.

Now I had a serious problem. For one thing, since we never put corpses in the freezer as a rule, and my technician had gone home, I didn't even know where the body was. Also, it turned out that Joyce lived just a few blocks from the clinic, so within minutes she was rushing through the front door in robe and curlers wanting to see Twinkle at once.

Twinkle, needless to say, was in no condition to be seen. By the time my receptionist paged me to come up front and console the weeping and wailing owner, I had located her in the freezer and she was a cat-sicle—frozen as solid as a hockey pond.

Trying to keep the panic out of my voice, I whispered over the phone to the receptionist, "Tell her we're trying emergency resuscitation and can't be disturbed. Put Joyce in an exam room at the very end of the hall, and assure her I'll be with her as quickly as I can."

What to do with Twinkle now? Ah, yes, there was the microwave we used to heat our coffee. Maybe four minutes on high would do the trick.

As you can imagine, that was a very long four minutes, indeed. I could picture Joyce wandering in about now, and me trying to explain what I was doing. But even after four minutes Twinkle was still as stiff as an ironing board. I tried twisting her joints a bit to loosen them up. They crackled and crunched sickeningly, but did finally loosen. Four more minutes on high might do the trick, I thought, peering intently through the glass microwave door fearing I'd see smoke.

When I removed her this time, she was at least limber and as warm as...toast. Much better. But as I turned to get a blanket to wrap her in, I heard a faint "ping...ping...ping," which turned out to be Twinkle's claws falling out one by one and bouncing around on the linoleum floor.

Even clawless, Twinkle was looking much better. But she was clearly having a bad hair day. Her fur was as wet and matted as if she'd just been taken from a washing machine. I sprinted for the grooming station and grabbed a hair dryer and brush. A few minutes of frantic postmortem grooming had her looking pretty decent, so I wrapped her in her special blanket, making sure all her toes were covered, took a deep breath, and headed for the exam room.

"Joyce," I said, wondering if I could somehow dim the room lights unobtrusively, "I'm sorry. We just lost her. I did everything I could."

"My poor, poor baby." Joyce was weeping quietly, rocking her blanket-wrapped cat gently back and forth in her arms. "She looks so good...like she's asleep. Are you sure she's gone?"

"Oh, yes, I'm sure—very sure." And I was also very sure that from that moment on, no matter how painful the situation was for me, I would always tell my clients exactly what was happening with their pets.

CHAPTER 2

You Are *Not* Necessarily What You Eat— Thank Goodness

"Could Schatzie have eaten anything unusual? Maybe the kids gave her something by mistake?" Schatzie, a normally feisty schnauzer, stood very still. She was hunched up like she'd swallowed a handful of razor blades and appeared to be in so much pain that she was afraid to twitch even the tip of her tail. I gently touched her belly. She shrieked.

My worried client shook her head emphatically. "No way. Absolutely not. We don't feed her anything except the food you prescribed. Ever." Her four children looked on silently while I continued my examination, which by every sign indicated severe digestive distress.

Just then, Schatzie began that rhythmic full body heaving that means breakfast is on the way back up. Ah, yes. There it was. A great pile of French fries, barely chewed, still ketchup-covered—an extra large bag by the look of it. The owner looked sheepish. "Well, I didn't...we really never...it just couldn't ...." She glared at the kids.

Dogs will eat almost anything—especially if their owners feed it to them. Unfortunately, some of these treats present serious health hazards. Any really fatty food such as French fries can cause pancreatitis in dogs. Pancreatitis, which was Schatzie's problem, is always very painful and can even be fatal. Other foods you might not expect, for instance chocolate, are straight out poisonous for dogs. Chocolate contains a chemical called theobromine, which can cause seizures and even heart attacks in dogs. Some kinds of chocolate, like baker's chocolate, have exceptionally high levels of theobromine. An ounce of baker's chocolate eaten by a small dog like a Chihuahua and it's curtains.

Cats are typically more sensible. Just because someone offers a cat a food item is no guarantee it will be eaten. Finicky eaters are usually sensible eaters.

If cats have a alimentary Achilles heel, it is anything that is long and stringy like ribbons or twine. No one knows why long stringy items appeal to cats' appetites. But as a consequence, the Christmas holidays are a time when veterinarians keep busy by surgically removing Christmas tree tinsel from cats. Tinsel, when swallowed, is very bad news. Generally, it balls up like yarn in the stomach and, as it moves into the intestines, can completely block the digestive tract. As if that isn't bad enough, sharp edges on the loose tendrils from the ball combined with the normal churning action of the intestines can slice like a saw through the intestinal wall, leading to fatal peritonitis.

This cat-tinsel problem has gotten even worse in recent years. It used to be that Christmas tinsel was actually made from metal so that it was easy to spot on an X ray. If diagnosed early enough, the cat can generally be saved by emergency surgery. Nowadays, though, tinsel is made from plastic. Since plastic doesn't show up on X rays, the problem is much harder to figure out. I guess all progress has its drawbacks.

Pet owners can be more directly responsible for their animals' dietary disorders than by just hanging tinsel on the tree. Daisy, for instance, was a yellow Labrador and, by definition then, a dog who liked to lick things. She would lick faces, hands, feet, bowls, floors, forks, tires, towels, walls, wool, virtually anything her tongue could reach. And she could reach a lot, because Julia, her owner, habitually encouraged Daisy to stand on her hind legs and give her sloppy kisses anytime she felt like it. By encouraging this behavior, of course, Julia was inadvertently training Daisy to rear and lick whenever the urge struck her. Once large dogs learn to rear, it is remarkable how many places in the house they can reach.

Julia's husband, a wealthy attorney, was not an animal person. He didn't like the licking, the rearing, dogs generally, and Daisy in particular. In fact, Julia was always worried that she would come home one day to find that her husband had run out of patience and hauled Daisy off to the pound. The husband felt like this even before the day when Daisy reared up to look for food on the kitchen drain board just after Julia had just set her large— really large—diamond wedding ring there while she washed dishes. Wouldn't you know it? *Slurp.* There went the wedding ring.

8

In my office, we X-rayed Daisy's stomach and sure enough there was the ring. I went over some treatment options. "The ring will probably pass," I explained, "so we could just wait a few days. If you watch her closely whenever she goes outside, you can probably get the ring pretty easily."

I was trying to be delicate. But I could tell from the look on Julia's face, that she was picturing exactly what "getting the ring back" this way entailed, and that the picture was not particularly appealing to her. "Or we could operate and get it back right now." Julia smiled. This was much better. Even though surgery is relatively expensive by veterinary standards, money was not a problem for Julia. Also, she would have the ring back immediately and would not have to worry that her husband might notice it was missing. And, even better, I would be the one who got to retrieve, and presumably clean, the ring.

In the meantime, Daisy was oblivious to the potential marital discord that her stomach contents represented. She pranced happily around my office while Julia and I talked, sniffing here, licking there, rearing up to check out what was on the counter. I moved some of my smaller instruments out of her reach. Then Daisy sidled up to Julia, perhaps to apologize in her fashion. She nudged Julia's hand. No response. Daisy probably thought that a little ingratiation was in order, so she reached up to give Julia's face a quick lick. *Slurp.* There went an earring, the one carat diamond stud her husband had purchased to match the wedding ring. It must have been loose anyway, but that was little consolation.

9

I managed to maintain my professional composure though it wasn't easy. We did operate after that, of course. We got back both the wedding ring and the earring without a problem. Daisy recovered nicely. Julie and I agreed on a story about an emergency spay to explain the surgical scar (and bill) to her husband. I never did learn how the marriage fared after that.

Sometimes, though, there is little that a pet owner can do to prevent their animal's digestive disorders. Take Benji Bitter, for instance. Benji was a poodle who as a puppy had catholic tastes. He ate anything, including rocks, buttons, pins, small toys, you name it. It got so that when the Bitters phoned for an appointment, the hospital staff would start making bets on what Benji had eaten now. As an adult though, Benji's taste matured. He developed what I can only describe as a food fetish. Lingerie was his particular specialty.

It was the panty hose that started him off, I think. The Bitters, like many of us, would, on occasion, leave yesterday's underwear lying around the house. Why Benji at some point decided that underwear was edible we will never know, but once he did there was no stopping him. I found the panty hose the first time I had to open him up. They were wadded up in his stomach with the legs sucked down into his intestines.

After that, it was an almost monthly occurrence. Underpants and socks usually passed through, although one sock might pass one day, the other the next. Negligées, panty hose, and undershirts usually didn't. Benji became a regular visitor to our operating room. He was costing his owners an arm and a leg so to speak. The Bitters grew meticulous about keeping their house tidy. No underwear on the floor—ever. But Benji was obsessed and all it took was one forgetful instant, a sock, a shirt absentmindedly thrown on a chair or sofa, and, *slurp*, it was gone.

The last time I saw Benji, he was in for the usual, an upset stomach, and hadn't eaten for several days, most likely due to a "foreign body" as we call them, which needed removing. By then Benji had become something of a hospital mascot. Everyone—receptionists, technicians, kennel help—greeted him effusively. Benji's owners had no idea what he had eaten this time. Nothing obvious was missing. But that wasn't particularly unusual. Unless you caught him in the act, how would you know?

On the operating table, we discovered the problem. A pair of woman's underpants had gotten lodged in his intestines. This was not a casual pair of underpants. These were black silk, embroidered, alluring, and obviously very expensive, like something out of a *Victoria's Secret* catalog. We decided to do our very good clients a favor. There were no tooth marks on the underpants. Benji must have swallowed them without chewing. Jan, my technician, suggested that she take them home, clean and iron them, and that we present them as a special surprise to the owners when they picked Benji up. And the next day that's just what we did.

"Dolly, Sam," I said to the owners, "all of us here at the hospital feel sorry that Benji has needed so much surgery over the past few months. So we are happy to be able, for once, to return these to you intact and as good as new." I handed them proudly to Dolly.

Dolly blushed. Then she began inspecting the underpants from one side, then the other. She held them up to the light, turning them over once again. "Sam," she finally said, giving her husband an icy stare, "do you mind telling me who these belong to?"

CHAPTER 3

Lazarus Turtles

Why people want turtles as pets is beyond me. Most people enjoy pets because of the emotional relationship that they can develop with their animals. The relationship doesn't have to be the sort of straightforward loyalty and affection that dogs can provide. Not all cats are affectionate, but cat owners can still chuckle at the aloof condescension with which their animals treat them. Snakes are not affectionate, but they can seem to be because they like to glide inside their owner's shirt or pants and coil around them to enjoy the body heat. But turtles? Not affectionate. Not intriguing personalities as a rule. In fact, the most frequent reason that turtle owners visit the veterinarian is to get a professional opinion about whether their pet is alive or not.

Marshall, a monstrous fifty pound turtle, had the closest thing I've seen to a turtle personality. He had been owned by the same woman for at least thirty-five years, so at least he'd had ample time to learn to recognize her. His dynamic turtle personality consisted of following her around and, at night, climbing unaided into a bottom dresser drawer, which she opened for him to sleep in. Of course despite what his owner thought, Marshall may have followed her around less from emotional attachment than from knowing his food source. He could have perceived her as a kind of mobile garden. Another client of mine owned more than thirty turtles, all of which lived in her backyard, and she was also sure that each turtle recognized and loved her. She thought this was so because every time she went out in the yard with a large tray of food, and her pets converged on her like ants converge on picnics. Her bubble was burst when she went out of town and hired a neighbor to feed this herd of turtles. The turtles converged on the neighbor with the same sluggish enthusiasm they usually showed her.

Turtles usually get sick because their owners don't know that they need real daylight, or they don't know what to feed them, or both. Without daylight, or exposure to specially manufactured "full spectrum" light bulbs, turtles, like most other animals, cannot make vitamin D. Without vitamin D, they won't absorb calcium, which causes a number of health problems, particularly soft bones.

The proper turtle diet depends on the type of turtle. Land-going turtles, which are usually called tortoises, tend to be fairly strict vegetarians, but aquatic turtles eat a fair amount of meat, such as snails, insect larvae, small fish, and worms, in addition to eating vegetation. If you don't feed your turtle the proper mixture of nutrients, it will develop a host of problems from soft shells to infectious diseases, primarily because of a suppressed immune system. You can now buy reasonably good turtle feed in many pet stores. But if your turtle is a terrestrial species, even this food should be supplemented with fruits and vegetables. Naturally, it helps to know whether your turtle is an aquatic or terrestrial type, because if you don't figure out the right food, it will soon be on its way to the veterinarian so that she can tell you whether or not it is still alive.

Even for a veterinarian though, providing an informed opinion about whether a turtle is alive is not trivial.

When they don't want to be disturbed for whatever reason, turtles retreat into their shells and batten down the hatches. They may do this because they are well-fed and just want to sleep, because it is getting cold and they are preparing to hibernate, because they are scared or ill, or just for the hell of it. This is the turtle version of locking yourself in a broom closet, turning off the lights, and trying to ignore the muffled sounds of the world outside. I appreciate how they feel, and sometimes wish I could do this myself.

Turtles don't have type-A personalities. Patience is their particular virtue. So once they withdraw into their shell, they may stay there for hours, even days. It is when they are ensconced inside their shells that determining whether they are dead or alive presents a challenge. No telling how many pet turtles have been buried, cremated, or pitched in a dumpster over the years because their owners falsely thought they were dead when, in fact, they were just chilling out in the broom closet.

Then there is the opposite error. During his internship, a former colleague of mine whom I'll call Dr. Beamer, unknowingly discharged a pet turtle from the hospital after it had already died. He gave the owner elaborate instructions about how to continue medical treatment of his pet at home. He explained how to give it injections by pulling one leg out from within the shell. He explained how many times a day to administer vitamins and subcutaneous fluids, and what to feed it until it was again well. The client kept looking at his pet, asking, "Are you sure he's still alive?" and my colleague kept assuring him it was just lethargic from the illness. It turned out it was lethargic from death. My colleague's embarrassment at this episode led him to invent what is still the best diagnostic test for a dead turtle, which I'll describe shortly.

Prior to my friend's test, there were several ways to try to determine whether a turtle was alive. I always preferred the water test. The water test consists of dropping the turtle into a tank of water and waiting to see whether it eventually comes up for air. Like I say, though, turtles are patience personified, so this test could take up much of a day. And naturally, if you leave the room for any reason, the turtle can always surface and resubmerge while you are gone. So the water test is time-consuming and not terribly accurate. I like it mainly because I can also use it to help diagnose whether the turtle has pneumonia. If it has pneumonia (and is alive), it will usually tilt to one side as it sinks and remain tilted on the bottom. If it is healthy and alive, or dead, or has pneumonia in both lungs, on the other hand, it sinks nice and straight—like a pet rock.

An alternative to the water test is the EKG test, which is quicker and more high tech, although not necessarily more accurate. This test consists of hooking a turtle up to an EKG, which records electrical activity of the heart. The idea is that if you get the classic flatline rather than the regular spikes of the heartbeat you can safely assume it's dead. This might seem a foolproof method, but it's not. The problem is that an EKG on a turtle is a bit more complicated than on a dog or cat or, for that matter, a human. For one thing, the heart of warm-blooded animals like dogs and cats and humans beats often—once to twice per second—so you never have to wonder whether you imagined the last beat or not, because another one is immediately on the way. A turtle's heart, on the other hand, particularly a sick turtle's heart, may beat once or twice *per minute*, usually just as you have looked away to scratch your nose.

Also, most people don't realize how sensitive an EKG is to disturbance. When a person is given an EKG, three or four flat disks attached to wires leading to the instrument are taped to her chest. The patient is then asked to breathe normally and not move. Not moving is important, because any slight movement of the wires causes false, chaotic spikes. With a dog or cat, you can't simply instruct them not to move, but with one to two heart beats per second, you can usually hold them still enough to evaluate a few undisturbed heart beats over the course of a few minutes.

Well, you obviously can't tape disks to the skin of a turtle which is withdrawn into its shell. To hook a turtle up to an EKG, you have to attach the wires to fine needles which you insert into the turtle wherever you can manage to reach beneath the shell. But the needles, not being taped in place, are exquisitely sensitive even to small vibrations. If someone slams a door somewhere down the hall, or laughs loudly, or stamps a foot, it may look on the EKG like the turtle's heart just beat. Imagine any place as busy as a veterinary hospital, where a few minutes can pass without someone slamming, laughing, pounding, or stomping somewhere in the building.

I once gave four of my new interns the job of determining whether a turtle was alive or not. These were all bright people, freshly out of vet school, brimming with confidence and energy. They thought I was kidding. Then they were insulted. Even a child can tell a dead animal from a live one. They obviously had had no experience with turtles. I left them alone for about thirty minutes and returned to find them clustered around the EKG, arguing. Two were certain it was dead. The other two were just as certain in was alive. They pointed to two recorded "heartbeats" on the chart recording. I looked at the turtle and clapped my hands. "There!" I said, "Another heartbeat. What do you think now?"

But now we have Beamer's test for a dead turtle, which makes all other tests obsolete. You can do this one at home. It takes no special training in the arcane arts of medicine. You don't have to watch your turtle for hours or days, and it is more accurate than anything your veterinarian is likely to do. First, lay the animal on a clean sheet of white paper. Then, using a sharp pencil, trace a precise outline around its shell on the paper. Wait forty-eight hours. If the shell is still precisely aligned with your tracing, or if no fewer than two legs are now outside the circle, assume it is dead. To be absolutely sure, though, repeat the test at least twice.

CHAPTER 4

I Don't Think We're Seeing Eye to Eye

Imagine this. You have gone off the road late at night on a lonely stretch of highway. You think you are seriously injured, but you're not sure how seriously. There are no phones or houses for miles, so your life probably depends on who happens upon the scene first. Would you feel luckier if that person was a veterinarian or a physician (or as we veterinarians like to say with a slight sneer, a *real* doctor)?

I contend you would be luckier if it were a veterinarian. Of course, veterinarians are not supposed to practice medicine on humans. There are legal prohibitions, and litigious consequences, if we do so. But think of it. Most human doctors hardly ever see patients for serious traumatic injuries. There are specialists for that. Ambulances and emergency medical technicians take trauma victims directly from accident scenes to emergency rooms, where there are physicians with special expertise in treating trauma. This is how it should be. But a consequence of this sort of specialization is that your average practicing physician has never likely treated a serious traumatic injury, unless it was during a rotation through the local emergency room back in medical school. Veterinarians, on the other hand, see patients with traumatic injuries nearly every day of their professional lives. Emergency medicine is as familiar to us as giving injections. And from a zoologist's point of view, one mammal is pretty much like another.

Don't get nervous. I don't practice medicine on humans. When we pass by car accidents, my husband invariably tries to discourage me from helping, unless there is no alternative. The potential legal consequences are too frightening.

However, I've never hesitated to practice on him. Particularly for minor problems. In fact, he insists on it— even after what I did to him when I was in vet school.

He had what was a trivial problem, really. One morning he awoke with a swollen lump under one of his eyes. It looked innocuous enough, something like the sort of goose egg you might get if you were punched in the eye. It wasn't bruised. It didn't interfere with his vision in any way. It just itched. We both thought it was likely some sort of allergic reaction, which would go away shortly. Unfortunately for him, I was taking veterinary ophthalmology at the time. It was a wonderful course, taught by Dr. Ron Riis, a world-famous veterinary ophthalmologist. Like a teenager with a new car, I was dying to try out my new knowledge. So we, or rather I, decided to treat his eye problem.

I came home with a bagful of medicated eye drops. I had fluorescin, a dye to tell me whether his cornea was damaged. I tried it. Neat. It worked. His cornea was fine.

I also gave him an anti-inflammatory and a drug called atropine. Atropine alleviates pain in an inflamed eye by relaxing certain muscles. He hadn't complained of pain, but I thought he might be just stoically ignoring it. I hated the thought that he might be in pain, so I gave him plenty of atropine. Besides, what's the use of trying out only a few of your new toys?

"Wait! What the hell. I can't see."

I stopped. "Of course you can't see, silly. I just put a bunch of drops in your eye. Wait a minute and it'll be fine."

I was wrong. Several minutes later, he still couldn't see. Actually, it wasn't that he couldn't see, but his vision was now blurred. If he looked out the eye I hadn't treated it was fine. The one I had treated was now blurry. One blurry eye and one good eye add up to blurry vision. As I thought about it, I realized that atropine works by relaxing eye muscles—paralyzing them. This was why his eye was now dilated, the iris muscles were paralyzed. "I bet things look really bright. Right?" I asked, hoping to convince him that I knew exactly what I had done.

"Bright and blurry," he said dejectedly.

Apparently, the atropine had paralyzed his lens muscles too. Lens muscles allow our eyes to focus on near or far objects. He now had one eye which was focusing normally, and another which was focused on infinity. By that evening, things were no better.

"How long will atropine be effective...er, in a dog?" I asked Dr. Riis as nonchalantly as I could the next day. He assured me that it wore off within twenty-four hours. So I expected that by the time I got home that evening, Steve's eye would be back to normal.

As I pulled into the driveway, I noticed that he was sitting on the porch, reading, with a hand over one eye. Not a good sign.

"What did he say?" he demanded rather grumpily.

"He said it should wear off within twenty-four hours."

"Well, it hasn't, has it?"

Puzzling. I thought about exactly what I had asked Dr. Riis, but came to the realization that what wears off within twenty-four hours in a dog wouldn't necessarily do so in a human.

"What if you accidentally got atropine on your surgical glove and accidentally rubbed your eye with it?" I asked Dr. Riis the next day.

"Whoa. Don't ever do that. That might be serious. You'd certainly have blurred vision for a while. I'm not sure how long. You'd have to ask a human doctor. Why?"

"Just curious." But I was more worried than curious. I hurried to the library to see what I could find out about atropine and humans.

It could be days was what the books said. They were right. Over the course of about ten days, Steve's vision did clear. He had no lasting effects. I'm the one with the lasting effects, because even now he never loses an opportunity to remind me of the therapeutic blindness I gave him.

My adventures with eyes were not over that semester. While still in the same ophthalmology course, my aunt Millie asked me if I would take care of her dog, Joel, while she drove to Florida to visit some old friends.

Millie was a wonderful person, the sort of kind and doting aunt for which everyone wishes. Joel was a Huck Finn kind of beagle. He had had a wild and independent puppyhood, living on his own in the Adirondack forest of upstate New York for God knows how long before Millie discovered him and gave him a comfy home indoors. Joel quickly became the focus of Millie's life. Her husband had died a few years previously, and living alone in a secluded house in the woods, Millie needed the companionship Joel provided. He was nice enough to people, but he never lost that rough edge. He would sometimes "go bush" as Steve called it, disappearing into the forest for several days, then returning as if nothing had happened. He also never lost the habit of eating any animals small and slow enough for him to catch. We knew he would eat mice, birds, rats, or cats, if given half a chance.

We had hardly any animals at home when I was in vet school, just our two dogs, Wart and Leo. We didn't worry about Joel eating them. Each was several times his size. We never thought for a second that my mother's miniature dachshund, Sebastian, could be a problem either, because Joel was in love with Sebastian.

Actually, all the other dogs were in love with Sebastian. That was the problem. They seemed to think that Sebastian, a castrated male with a petulant and coquettish way about him, was really a female. And he did nothing to dissuade them of this belief.

Male dogs, like male humans, tend to go a bit crazy around attractive females, and our dogs were no exception. One day as we were walking all the dogs in the woods, Joel and Leo each suddenly decided that Sebastian was his girl, and the next thing you know, all hell broke loose. We didn't see whether Joel first jumped Leo, or vice versa, but there was a sudden whirling mass of dogs, a blur of teeth and blood and fur, and a cacophony of snarling and shrieking. Ninety-nine out of a hundred quick dog fights like this end with nothing more than a scrape here or a hole there. But of course, in a fight between my dog and my sweet aunt's dog, the hole happened to be right through Joel's eye. The eye was destroyed. What would I say to Aunt Millie?

We had been talking about prosthetic eyes in class. These cosmetic replacements for real eyes had been used in humans for years, but were just coming on the market in 1982 for dogs. Before prosthetics, dogs' or cats' eyes damaged by disease or injury were usually removed and the lid sewn shut. But animals lose some of their facial expressiveness when one of their eyes is permanently closed, so there was a demand for a better solution. Prosthetic eyes. The technology was so new, and so seldom used in traumatic injuries, that I thought (I hoped) the case of sufficient interest that Dr. Riis would come in on a weekend to try surgically implanting one in Joel. It had to be done right away because of infection.

Prosthetic eyes don't look like real eyes. The shell of the old eye is left, but the colored part of the eye, the iris and pupil, is removed and replaced by what is essentially a black marble. This would look truly spooky in a human, because the white of our eye takes up most of what we see and the iris and pupil stand out in stark contrast. A prosthetic eye would make any of us look like some sort of space alien. So for cosmetic and psychological reasons, people with a prosthetic eye usually wear a contact lens with an iris and pupil painted on.

Dogs' eyes are a little different though. Look at your dog. There is no visible white of the eye. It is *all* iris and pupil. A prosthesis in a dog looks much more like a real eye, dilated to the max. Well, okay, it doesn't look all that much like a real eye. Still it sort of, maybe, looks something like an real eye and maybe Millie, whose vision wasn't the sharpest, wouldn't notice.

Dr. Riis was a prince. He agreed to come in immediately and do the surgery. I paid, of course, by being the butt of an endless stream of jokes during the surgery. "Your Aunt Millie won't notice, riiiigght. Think she'd notice if we took off a leg?" "How about a patch and a parrot and we'll call him Long John Silver?" And so on.

But it didn't look all that bad when we got Joel back. It certainly didn't seem to affect him much. Joel was ready to go after Leo again right away. Dogs don't rely on their eyes like we do. In fact, people frequently bring dogs to the veterinarian for other reasons, only to be told that their dog has been completely blind from glaucoma or some other disease for weeks or months. Dogs get by quite well using their nose and memory. Just watch out if you move the furniture around.

When Millie returned, we said nothing. I didn't want to deny what happened, but I didn't want to bring it up unnecessarily either. So we acted as if nothing had happened, and to our relief so did Millie. A couple of months later though, I spoke to my mother. "You won't believe what Millie told me," she said.

"Oh, oh," I thought.

"She told me Joel must have had some sort of accident when he was with you. One of his eyes is gone. She thought maybe you hadn't noticed, and didn't want to embarrass you by pointing it out." And that's what made Aunt Millie so wonderful.

CHAPTER 5

A Pig's Best Friend

Some exotic pet fads you can understand. Sugar gliders, those flying squirrel-like marsupials that are the current rage, are cute. Being nocturnal, they have those huge soft eyes like children in the paintings of Walter Keane. Earlier fad species, like ferrets, iguanas, and hedgehogs, I could see appealing to certain types of people. But I never could figure out how pot-bellied pigs became such popular pets in the mid-1980s.

Pot-bellied pigs are pretty much like other pigs, just a lot smaller—no heavier than a large dog with very short legs. Small enough, in other words, to live in your house or apartment, flop on your couch, or sleep in your bed. Maybe people thought that pigs didn't shed. But they actually do. Real pigs are not as bald as cartoon pigs. They shed hairs that are not as long, and coarse, and prickly as porcupine quills, but it's long, and coarse, and prickly enough to lodge under your skin. They don't bark, which is an advantage, but they do grunt and squeal ceaselessly.

Pigs are smart. Maybe that was part of it too. Most people have no idea how smart pigs are. You can house-train a pig. They will learn to ring a bell with their nose when they need to go outside, and ring again when they want to come back in. If you live in an apartment, you can train your pig to use a litter box. Well, I guess it wouldn't be a litter box exactly. More like a litter tub. You can train them to walk on a leash too. When we lived in Venezuela, we even had a pet pig, Adobo, who learned to beg for mangoes by sitting like a dog.

Probably the best test of an animal's intelligence is not what it can be trained to do, but what it can learn on its own. Pigs are certainly not the quickest and most agile of creatures, but I know of at least two pigs who figured out how to catch small birds.

These were not pet pigs, but barnyard pigs. They belonged to a farmer who had struck a deal with the manager of a nearby biscuit manufacturing plant to purchase the plant's waste dough to use as pig feed. This waste dough was delivered by the truckload—seventeen-ton lots—unbaked biscuits the size of bungalows. With such a high carbohydrate diet, the pigs apparently decided they needed to supplement their rations with a little protein. So they soon learned to eat tunnels into the dough, hide out inside the tunnels, and ambush unsuspecting birds when they arrived for a bit of biscuit. These pigs gobbled starlings like they were bonbons.

The birds did not sit well with the pigs' digestive system, which brings up one of the disadvantages of pigs as pets. They eat like, well, pigs. That is, they eat often, and they eat anything. For such a gourmandizing species, pigs have surprisingly delicate stomachs. In fact, most of the veterinary problems suffered by pot-bellied pigs are due to their stomachs in one way or another. So the first medical advice I give pig owners is to always have an extra large bottle of Pepto-Bismol on hand. I also tell them to use a dash of common sense about what they feed their animal. Don't feed pigs pizza. Don't feed them boxes of cheese snacks or expensive steaks. For heaven's sake, don't feed them pork. In fact, don't feed them table scraps period. Stick to commercial diets. Pet pig pellets, not commercial pig pellets (which are designed to make them gain weight as quickly as possible). An indoor pig with a bad case of gastroenteritis, vomiting and diarrhea in nontechnical language, is not a pretty sight or sound or smell.

You need to watch how much you feed them too. Pigs, if given the opportunity, will become obese beyond imagining—literally too obese to stand or see. A pig will eat until it is heavier than its legs can support. Before it reaches that stage, however, that fetching fat pad on its forehead will grow until it droops down over its eyes.

Even if you watch their diet like Dr. Pritikin, there are other problems you can have with your pet pig. For one thing, don't forget that what pigs like to do best outdoors is to root and wallow. They root just in case there is any food to be found, churning the earth like a roto-tiller gone berserk. They wallow for the sheer joy of it, whenever they have rooted out a large enough crater.

When I practiced in a Boston suburb, one of my clients, let's call him Frank, came into an inheritance and used a fair fraction of it to turn the two acres surrounding his house into a garden worthy of Kubla Khan. His landscaper put in grassy knolls, exotic shrubs, prize-winning flowers, and a fish pond that might have come from a Norman Rockwell painting. Draining from the pond was a small stream straddled by a miniature wooden bridge painted bright red. Having grown up a city boy, Frank decided that this bucolic scene lacked only a pig to complete it. So he purchased a personable young pot-bellied pig and named it Hamilton (Ham, for short. What else?). Within a day his garden looked pretty much like it had come under heavy artillery attack. The shrubs were stripped, the flowers gone, the stream fouled, the lawn devastated. Ham was happy as could be. He stretched out on his side in a muddy wallow atop one grassy knoll, grunting contentedly.

Most people would have been furious—at the pig or more appropriately at themselves. But pig owners, in my experience, are an indulgent lot. Once people grow attached to them, pigs can do no wrong. Even in New Guinea, where life in the bush is harsh and pigs are thought of more as protein on the hoof than pets in a traditional sense, my husband has seen village women nurse baby pigs from their own breasts, and carry them around as they would their own nursing infants. Frank was not about to go that far. He was clearly not happy about his garden, but he didn't talk about turning Ham into ham either. JoAnn, another client, was even more attached than Frank to her pot-bellied boar. Pig people are less than imaginative about names. Her boar was Ham(ilton) too.

Pot-bellied boars are considerably rarer as pets than pot-bellied sows, because boars have a well-deserved reputation for growing aggressively territorial after puberty. *Your* house gradually becomes *their* house. For a while, it even looked like a guard boar industry might develop.

31

Who wants to mess with a two-foot high, 150-pound tank with tusks? It never worked out, though, because boars just couldn't be trained to be discriminating about who they would allow in their territory. They allow no one in except rutting sows. Few people turned out to be thrilled about an exotic guard pet that wouldn't allow them inside their own home.

You can usually overcome the territory problem by castrating boars when they are young. Then you have a nice, smart, loyal pet, like JoAnn's Ham. But Ham developed another problem that is relatively common in pot-bellied pigs—bladder stones.

Okay, Ham had bad skin too, but all indoor pigs have bad skin. Scabies is a skin disease caused by an allergic reaction to the eggs and feces of a burrowing mite. When infested with scabies mites, people or pigs break out in small, itchy, pustulating sores all over, particularly around the ankles. If one scabies mite is stranded alone somewhere in your county, it will find your indoor pig, begin making baby mites, and soon infest everyone in the household.

"JoAnn, enough pussyfooting around. I think we need to solve this problem once and for all." I ignored Ham's scabies to concentrate on his bladder stones. Cats are prone to bladder stones too. There are a zillion theories about what causes them, but no one really knows. When a stone develops in males, it eventually lodges in the urethra, that long tube leading from the bladder to the tip of the penis, blocking urination. It is excruciatingly painful. Even relatively inattentive pet owners notice when their animal screams and strains mightily while unsuccessfully trying to urinate.

Ham wasn't screaming now. He was out cold—anesthetized—and I was inserting a catheter (a plastic tube) into his urethra to try to unblock him. It felt like I was pushing it through ground glass. "Remember that surgery I told you about?" I said to JoAnn as she absentmindedly scratched her wrist with one hand, her neck with the other.

There is a simple permanent surgical solution to the bladder stone problem. We do it all the time in tomcats. It goes by the intimidating medical name of perineal urethrostomy, but consists of nothing more than amputating the penis and enlarging the urethral opening where it comes out of the body wall. For cats, life after the surgery is pretty much the same as life before the surgery, only now it's pain-free. For pigs, the situation is a little more complicated.

The difference between cats and pigs is that male cats have muscles inside their body, which allow them to open and close their urethra at will. So they can urinate when and where they choose, even without a penis. Boars, on the other hand, control urination with muscles inside the penis itself. So after the same surgery, they become incontinent, like a leaky faucet. I try to avoid the surgery in pigs until I'm convinced that their stones will keep returning. Twice already, I'd left Ham's external anatomy intact and removed his stones by opening up his bladder. This was strike three.

For boars and boar owners, a perineal urethrostomy

isn't necessarily a catastrophe. If it was an outdoor pet before, life goes on unchanged. If it was an indoor pet, it becomes an outdoor pet. Or so I thought.

Several months after Ham's operation, one of JoAnn's best friends brought her own pig to me for a routine check-up. I asked her how JoAnn and Ham were adapting. She looked puzzled. Adapting? "I mean after the surgery. The incontinence. Have they worked it out?"

A light went on. Her face brightened. "Oh, the rubber sheets solved the problem."

Now I was puzzled. "Rubber sheets?"

"Sure. Wasn't that a good idea? I mean they were miserable for a while. JoAnn had to do something. Ham just wouldn't tolerate diapers, and those king-size mattresses are expensive. She was going broke replacing it so often. Rubber sheets were a stroke of genius, weren't they? Things are fine now."

CHAPTER 6

Down and Almost Out

"Whoa, is your dog's breath foul. He's fat too. Anything else wrong with him?"

I could hear Miss Mazet loud and clear even though there was at least one hundred feet and several walls between me and the waiting room, where some poor soul had just had the misfortune to have Miss "Don't-Call-Me-Julie" Mazet plop down next to her.

She wasn't finished either. "So am I. Fat, I mean. What the hell, so are you. Look at us. Two fatsos with fat pets. Ha! At least we know what we're doing to ourselves. You should feed that dog less, you know that? Take it from me, that's what the doctor will tell you. Slim him down and he'll be fine. Don't bother to thank me for the free advice, no one else does."

I couldn't hear what Miss Mazet's victim said in response. It usually didn't matter. She would continue on regardless of what you said. "Well, he looks fine to me, and I can tell when an animal is sick. Your dog isn't sick, just too fat. Have any idea how much vets make off those tests? Talk about sick. You don't know sick. My Binky is sick, really sick. He's still alive, though, no thanks to these quacks. He's alive because of me. You'd never do for your dog what I do for my Binky. No one would."

Many of us go into veterinary medicine, as opposed to human medicine, because of the belief that as animal doctors we won't have to deal with complicated, nonmedical, people problems. We think we will be able to devote all our energies to providing our silent and grateful patients with the finest medical care. This is a ridiculously juvenile and naïve notion, of course. We seem to get all the people problems that human doctors get, plus our patients can't tell us how they are feeling. We get no training in people problemology either. We either figure it out on our own or go into another profession.

Miss Mazet was my introduction to just how complicated people problems could get. I was a senior vet student at the time, just beginning to work up my own cases, but still with backup from Cornell's veterinary teaching faculty. Sometimes an instructor would peer right over your shoulder as you performed your physical examination. But more often, especially for those of us who were already comfortable with the clinical basics, instructors would leave you on your own, trusting that you would shout for help if you needed it. It wouldn't have done you any good to shout for help when Miss Mazet was in the building, though. When she arrived, all instructors magically disappeared. That should have been a tip-off.

What made dealing with Miss Mazet such a challenge was that she had a knack, a gift, maybe even a genius, for the irritating comment. She could get under your skin like a picador. Her only saving grace, the sole thing that kept us all from flat-out refusing to deal with her, was her total dedication to her cat, Binky. Given that grating personality, the cat was probably Miss Mazet's only friend in the world. But her devotion was so pure and apparent that you couldn't help but respect it.

Respecting her devotion made her no easier to deal with though. When I first encountered her, she was coming to the clinic every day for Binky's treatment. Her visits had quickly become noted events, in the same way that earthquakes are noted events. She would march through the front door bright and early, complaining loudly, and almost immediately begin to pester whoever happened to occupy the chair next to wherever she decided to sit. This signaled the faculty to evaporate, leaving us senior students to handle her and the string of irate clients she left in her wake, all on our own. She was so outlandishly and consistently obnoxious, that stories about "The Maz," as we called her (whenever we were certain she couldn't overhear us), became eagerly anticipated highlights of vet student gatherings at The Caboose, a local pub where we congregated during those few hours we weren't working clinics, studying for board exams, or sleeping.

The reason Miss Mazet came in every day was not specifically to torture us. It was that Binky was indeed really sick. He was an ancient blue-eyed Siamese cross with a laundry list of health problems. But the worst problem, the one that was killing him, was kidney failure. His kidneys were shot, permanently. There was no chance he would ever get any better. The only way to keep him alive, even for a short while, was to drip intravenous fluids and medications into him for most of his waking hours. After a while, his veins were so badly scarred that you could hardly find one. It might take ten minutes or more of repeated jabbing before you got a needle successfully into a vein. Finally his only lifeline became the Teflon tube we had to permanently install in his jugular vein. This was not a high quality of life to be sure, but euthanasia was not an option. Any mention of it earned you several minutes of sustained abuse from Binky's owner, who knew how to dish it out.

Faithfully, every morning Miss Mazet showed up to sit with Binky while he was getting these treatments, murmuring to him, and rocking him gently back and forth for the rest of the day as he lay in his personal pram amid fluid bags, tubes, and needles. Binky's pram was no ordinary pram. It was as white and frilly as a queen's canopy bed and so finely engineered that you could probably have set a full wine glass among its pillows and pushed it across train tracks without spilling a drop.

The saga of Binky and Miss Mazet was sad, of course, but it had its amusing side too, once you were away from her. Creative abuse is, after all, fun to observe as long as you are not in the firing line. Any amusement vanished for good, though, the afternoon I walked in to the exam room to check Binky's IV and found Miss Mazet and her cat both stretched out unconscious with plastic laundry bags firmly tied over their heads.

Like I say, we got no training in people problems, so I followed my first instinct which was to turn and walk right back out of the room. This situation clearly required help from an instructor. That's what they were there for, right? For when we knew we were in over our heads.

Fortunately, just outside in the corridor I stumbled into Dr. Exner, who must not have heard that The Maz was in the building. Ex, as we called him, was a superb teacher. Portly, with horn-rimmed spectacles and a reddish Santa Claus beard, he was known among the students for his calm patience and willingness to explain in detail every procedure and clinical decision even as he worked. This time his calm patience was not what I needed. I breathlessly explained the situation. "What do you think we should do?" he said calmly.

"We?" I thought, "We? I'm just a student. You're the doctor. I'm not supposed to become all-knowing and all-wise until after June when I graduate. You're supposed to be that way now."

We both shook off our mental paralysis at about the same moment. He shouted to the reception desk to call for an ambulance, and we ran back into the room together. Ripping the bag off Miss Mazet's head, we determined that she was still breathing at least. Her tongue and gums were blue, but her pulse was strong. We began to shake her gently. We patted her face, trying to bring her to consciousness. I wondered whether a bucket of cold water in the face, like in the movies, might be justified. Shortly, she did begin to come around. "Binky," she moaned. "Where's Binky?"

We had forgotten about Binky. Ripping the bag off *his* head, we saw that he was alive, but very blue, very comatose, barely breathing, and in a very bad way indeed.

Ex and I looked at each other. I thought about what Binky had been through, what his prospects were. "D...N...R?" I silently mouthed. This is doctortalk for *Do Not Resuscitate*. Ex nodded. "Binky's gone," he told her gently. "Don't try to get up. Breathe slowly and deeply. The ambulance is on its way." I unhooked Binky from his IVs and carried him out of the room to die quietly elsewhere.

In thinking about this episode many years later, trying to sort out what it taught me, a couple of things stand out. First, I'm not particularly proud of the way I handled things. I wish now that I'd been more patient and persistent about explaining Binky's situation to Miss Mazet, been able to ignore her abuse long enough to get my points across. Maybe I would have got through to her eventually. Maybe we could have painlessly euthanized him, worked through her grief together, found her a new cat, and avoided the ensuing catastrophe.

One thing I don't regret is letting Binky die. Even today, I almost never give up on an animal if there's hope. If anything, I'm too much the other way. I often continue working on animals that everyone else thinks are hopeless. Some of my proudest moments have come as I've watched these animals, the so-called "goners," walk out of the hospital under their own power and go home. So I trust it carries extra weight when I say that the case of Miss Mazet and Binky, plus many cases I've handled since, have convinced me that DNR orders are not used nearly enough in veterinary medicine. We try to resuscitate way too many animals.

It's one thing if a healthy animal happens to have a cardiac arrest during a spay or some other minor procedure. Of course, you do everything you can to resuscitate it. If you're successful, it will probably have no lasting effects and lead a normal life afterward. On the other hand, if an animal is in the hospital for what we call organic disease, which basically means cancer or other diseases of the brain, heart, liver, or kidney, resuscitating it after an arrest is a bad clinical and humanitarian decision. To determine exactly how bad, I recently went back through the medical records of all the hundreds of such resuscitation attempts that have taken place during the past twenty years at the hospital where I currently work, the Washington State Veterinary Teaching Hospital.

Because it is a teaching hospital full of highly trained specialists, animals are likely to get considerably more skilled care there than at a normal clinic. Even so, I found exactly one case among these hundreds with organic disease in which an animal was resuscitated and recovered enough to go home alive. We put animals and owners through a lot of physical or emotional suffering, and build up false hopes for, at best, a few hours to few days of low-quality existence. These measures aren't just futile; they are expensive. We charge $200 just to start resuscitation and it goes up quickly from there.

I suppose this is a long-winded way of apologizing for the lie we told Miss Mazet. Binky was still alive, barely, even when the EMT's rolled her gurney out of the hospital and lifted it into ambulance. But he died peacefully soon afterward.

41

I also learned that you can't have standardized general rules for specific medical cases. There is no standard way to handle a standard illness. Cases may be medically identical, but emotional relations between pets and their owners never are. You can't be a good veterinarian without trying to understand these emotional ties, and working your knowledge of them into the way you manage treatment. I try not to classify them as good or bad, healthy or sick relationships, but just different ones, each with its own logic. Who am I to say, for instance, that Miss Mazet was mentally unbalanced, or was wrong to try to kill herself over her pet's terminal illness? I can't say that with any more certainty than I could say that Romeo was wrong to kill himself over Juliet. I have no special insight to how desolate and desperate her particular life may have become without Binky for company. I should have thought about this more when trying to figure out how to deal with the two of them.

I never saw Miss Mazet again. I graduated not long after that and went off to New Mexico to become a real world doctor. Before I left, I did hear that she had recovered, at least physically, and gone home from the hospital. If she got herself a new cat, she may be terrorizing some of my student successors today. That should keep them on their toes.

CHAPTER 7

The (Imagined) Emotional Lives of Animals

Animals have emotions and feelings. I'm sure they feel something akin to joy, anger, grief, and who-knows-what-else. Only fools, people who have never owned or observed pets, and certain breeds of academic animal behaviorists doubt the very existence of animal emotions. We don't necessarily understand much about these emotions, but it's difficult to deny their existence.

Some people imagine, though, that if animals have emotional lives, they must have the same kind of emotional lives we do. The same attitudes, impulses, and hang-ups, in other words, of middle class Americans in the twenty-first century. Such people project their own emotions onto their pets. I once had a client, call her Susan, who wanted me to vasectomize her cat Emmett instead of castrating him, the usual procedure for sterilizing males. Her rationale was that as a responsible pet owner she wanted him sterilized, but she also wanted him to lead a normal cat's emotional life. A tomcat's testicles are so prominent a feature of his appearance, she told me, that without them he'd be too embarrassed to continue hanging out with his street corner buddies and might lack confidence around the ladies.

I managed to talk her out of the vasectomy and into a standard castration with a bit of effort, but I had a much tougher time talking her out of euthanizing the same perfectly healthy cat just a few months later. She thought he was a failed suicide, terminally depressed. If he couldn't quite go through with ending his own life, she, as his devoted owner, felt duty-bound to assist him. Call her Susan Kevorkian, I thought to myself.

It's probably obvious by now that Susan loved animals dearly, but didn't understand them at all. She lived in New York City most of the time, but had recently purchased a country house not far from where I was practicing in upstate New York. This house was her retreat from the pressure and pace of the city, a place to dream about a perfect world of natural harmony, where the lion could lie down with the lamb, the dog with the cat, the cat with the rat, the motor vehicle with the dog. I mention this last item, because her view of the countryside was so suffused with rosy unreality that when visiting her country home, she refused to keep her animals indoors or confine them to her fenced yard, even though having been raised in her Manhattan apartment, they hadn't a clue about avoiding vehicles, not to mention other rural dangers such as coyotes, owls, and mountain lions in which New York City is decidedly deficient. They needed to enjoy nature unfettered, she told me.

At the time, she only had two pets, thank God. Her dog Wolfie, a schnauzer named after Wolfgang Amadeus

44

Mozart, had been with her since he was a puppy. She had no problem with castrating him, because he never hung out with other dogs, just with her. As Wolfie grew into adulthood, spending each day locked inside her apartment while she was at work, she gradually became convinced that he must be leading a lonely, deprived existence. I'm sure it never occurred to her that he probably slept 95 percent of the time that she was gone. Or that with his myriad toys and regular evening walks, plus the constant attention she lavished on him when she was home, he likely got more than enough companionship to keep him emotionally satisfied. He certainly got far more attention than many pets do.

To cure his imagined loneliness, she decided he needed an animal friend to keep him company. This wasn't a bad idea whether he was really lonely or not. However, it wasn't such a great idea to get a cat to be his pal rather than another dog. Her rationale was that Wolfie would feel less displaced in her affections if the new animal in the house was another species, something like a child might feel less displaced, if a family got a dog as opposed to a new baby. Therefore she acquired Emmett, a yellow tabby, at about the same time that she purchased her new country house in my neighborhood.

It was bound to happen, of course. Not long after I castrated Emmett, Wolfie, while enjoying nature, free and unfettered, was run over and killed by a delivery truck. At least it was quick. Taking a direct shot from a sizable vehicle doing the speed limit, he didn't suffer. Susan was understandably shaken up. Maybe she needed to reassess the beautiful simplicity of animals' lives in the country-side. She began to surreptitiously observe Emmett as he went about his daily business outdoors, attempting to understand what life in the countryside was really like for him. After a few days she came to me to ask if I would euthanize poor Emmett.

I couldn't help but scold her. "Listen, Susan, I under-stand that you're upset about Wolfie, but I can't put down a perfectly healthy cat just because you suddenly lost your taste for owning animals."

"It's not that, Dr. K. No. I still love Emmett and want the best for him. But he's so upset since Wolfie died. Do you know what I saw him do? Twice I watched him walk right out in front of speeding cars, and jump back only at the last second. He wants to kill himself. I just know it. But he can't quite make himself do it. His courage fails at the last second. God, he must be so miserable without Wolfie."

It was time to lay some things on the line. I probably should have done so earlier, but I hadn't wanted to burst her bucolic bubble. That day had not been an easy one anyway. I'd already lost a couple of animals that I had worked desperately hard to save and I wasn't in a mood for someone to ask me to purposely kill her healthy pet. "Wait a minute, Susan. First of all, Emmett doesn't under-stand cars any more than you would if you had been raised in the jungle by wolves. He understands apart-ments, couches, coffee tables. He walks out in front of cars because he doesn't know any better. At the last minute, he realizes something very large and very fast is about to smash into him, so he jumps out of the way. You're lucky he's still young and quick. Second of all, as I recall, you couldn't leave Wolfie and Emmett in the same room together unless you were there, right? You were afraid Wolfie might kill him. He even tried it a couple of times in front of you, yes? Does this sound like a pal Emmett would get suicidally depressed over? Think about it. Keep your cat inside, he'll be your good friend and companion for a long time. Keep letting him roam around here, and you won't have to ask me to put him down for you much longer."

Susan looked stricken and I immediately felt sorry for my outburst. She did change her mind, however. She took Emmett home and turned him into a full-time house and apartment cat. So far as I know, he subsequently led a long and happy life of confinement.

Not all housebound pets lead happy, well-adjusted lives though. Emotions of both pets and owners can sometimes go a bit off track. It's always easy to blame the owner when a pet seems a little nutty, and owners are often at fault. But if we grant that animals have emotions, there is no reason to think they can't develop emotional problems and neuroses on their own, just like people can. Some dogs, for instance, get what we call separation anxiety, in which they go a bit mad whenever their owners leave them alone in the house. I remember treating a German shepherd for severe lacerations, because instead of trying to claw his way through the kitchen door as he normally did when his owners left for work, he decided to jump through the bay window and follow after them.

Although it's hard to imagine how the behavior of pet owners could bring about that kind of anxiety, it's easy to see how they could make it worse. The owners of the lacerated shepherd, for instance, instead of getting some professional advice, began taking their dog along with them whenever he raised a particularly big fuss. True, it saved wear-and-tear on the kitchen door, but it also reinforced in the dog the idea that if it made a desperate enough attempt to break out of the house, it was likely to be taken along. So the owners may have been partly responsible for that leap through the front window. There are specialists in animal behavioral therapy who can often help in such cases. Also, we have pretty decent success in treating these types of problems with the same drugs used for helping manage human anxiety.

A stranger type of animal neurosis, something that is also hard to pin on pet owners, is an unreasonable addiction to a specific routine. My favorite case of this sort was a pharaoh dog, a rare breed which looks something like a small greyhound, named Ramesses that would allow his owner to leave the house once each day without any problem, but he wouldn't allow the owner to leave twice. This owner, who was a pharmacist as I recall, lived near his workplace. If he simply left for work in the morning and came home at night, all was fine. But if for some reason he returned during the day to grab a bite to eat or retrieve something that he had forgotten that morning, when he left the second time his dog destroyed something—a couch, a chair, a bed. When I say destroyed, I don't mean it nipped off a piece here or there; I mean Ramesses tore the thing to bits. This created a certain amount of anxiety in the owner too, who knew if he had to return home during the day for any reason, there would be severe consequences. I thought this might turn out to be a rare instance where a neurotic pet drove an owner crazy, rather than the reverse.

I tried the usual treatment first. Ramesses still had all his reproductive equipment, so I castrated him. This seldom works, although it is the standard initial treatment, probably due to remnant attitudes from the days when lots of superstitions surrounded hormones. Hormone injections years ago were thought to be able to rejuvenate the sex drive of aging men and even slow the aging process itself. And women suffering from what was known at the time as hysteria could supposedly be cured by hysterectomies.

But like I say, it seldom works. It didn't work in this particular case either, so I suggested something very simple. Let's try confining Ramesses to a portable kennel during the day, I said. We probably should have tried that first, but there are lots of other good reasons—improved health, longer life—to sterilize your animal anyway, so I didn't feel too bad about it. When confined in the kennel however, the dog's anger or anxiety or whatever it was, turned inward. Ramesses chewed off all his toenails and began eating his feet. Finally, we tried anti-anxiety drugs, but in this case, they didn't work. At last we admitted defeat, and the owner reluctantly found Ramesses a new home with a retired couple, who never both left the house at the same time.

Oddly, some species are more prone than others to turning their emotions inward like Ramesses in his kennel. Cats, by contrast, are more likely to turn them outward, to go on the attack when anxious or upset. The classic case is new baby syndrome. Susan, as it turns out, wasn't completely off her rocker to worry about the psychological effects on Wolfie of bringing a new animal into the house. When a new baby arrives in a household, family cats, especially those used to a lot of attention, are sometimes disturbed enough to turn from well-behaved, litterbox-trained lap cats to madly scratching, biting, urinating fiends. They tend to urinate right where, from their perspective, the problem lies—in the baby's crib, on the baby's blanket, even on the baby itself. You might call this jealousy or defending one's territory or watching out for number one. We don't know the human emotion to which it is most similar. There is quite obviously some sort of internal emotional turmoil though.

Some emotional problems of animals look just like physical problems. I think of Max, a golden retriever that I was convinced had a brain tumor. His owner had brought him to me because he spent his life turning round-and-round in circles, counterclockwise. Sure enough in my exam room as soon as his leash was removed, he turned and looked over his left shoulder, then began trotting in counterclockwise circles about the size of a couch. His owner and I watched him do this steadily for at least five minutes. I decided to see if I could disrupt the pattern by standing directly in his path. Nope. He just moved farther away and continued. I crowded him a bit more. He kept circling even when having to bounce off the wall.

What would happen if I worked him into a corner? The corner stopped him. He couldn't figure out what to do. He kept looking over his left shoulder and hopping back and forth from one front foot to the other. I moved back, but now he was hung up in the corner and so just continued bouncing from foot to foot. The bouncing eventually backed him away from the corner to the point where he could start circling again, and this is just what he did. The owner had even brought in a videotape of his retriever at home. There he was circling to the left in the living room. The owner's voice-over was saying, "Ten o'clock, still circling....Two, still at it...Five, he hasn't stopped yet..." and so on.

Obsessive circling behavior is a classic sign of a brain lesion, usually a tumor. This looked to me like a classic left brain lesion. Fortunately, we have a world-class neurologist on our staff. I wanted his opinion. He could no doubt locate the tumor pretty precisely with a more sophisticated battery of tests. I also knew he would be fascinated by the case. I explained to the owner that he would have to leave Max overnight so that our neurologist could perform a thorough examination in the morning. We put Max in a heavily padded run so he wouldn't bang himself up while circling for hours, and put a large sign on the run explaining his problem. I didn't need students and technicians interrupting me all day to ask did-I-know-that-retriever-in-back-was-circling-in-its-run-and-never-stopped?

I was interrupted anyway. Molly, one of my brightest students, stuck her head in an exam room as I was talking with a client. "Dr. K. did you know the retriever in the padded run is…"

"Yes," I interrupted her, not happy at being disturbed when I was with a client and overrun with cases anyway. "I know. He circles. Didn't you see the sign?"

She looked hurt. "I *did* see the sign. I just wanted to let you know he isn't circling. Hasn't been all afternoon. He's…"

"Thanks for the information, Molly. Please wait outside and we'll talk it over when I'm finished here." I finished up with my client, then hurried with Molly out to the kennels.

There indeed sat Max, looking eager and excited, surrounded by senior vet students, adoring the attention. Wanting to confirm his miraculous cure, I took him into an exam room by myself. He stood there calmly looking at me. "Sit, Max." He sat. "Lie down." He lay down. "Come here." He approached, tail wagging. I scratched him under the chin.

Stranger things have happened. Occasionally someone brings in a very sick animal, we perform all sorts of tests, never really identify what the problem is, but it goes away anyway, without treatment. This makes us look very smart. We try to make it sound impressive. "Well, we had spontaneous remission of that idiopathic syndrome," which is medical jargon for, "We have no idea what the problem was, but it seems to have disappeared on its own."

I phoned Max's owner, who hurried in to fetch his dog. He was relieved, of course, to be spared an exhaustive and expensive neurological evaluation, but even more relieved to have a well animal. I went through the idiopathic syndrome bit with him, then asked my technician to get Max. He pranced in friskily, heeling nicely for the technician, took one look at his owner, looked over his left shoulder, and began circling and circling, counter-clockwise.

I was at a loss. What could make the owner's presence set off such behavior? I suggested the owner see our behavioral therapist, which he did. The therapist, who quizzed Max's owner for hours, couldn't figure out why his presence set off such behavior in Max either. She did diagnose Max as having obsessive-compulsive disorder, the same sort of neurological problem that causes some people to obsess with anxious thoughts so that they wash their hands, or check that the oven is turned off, three hundred times per day. Drugs have been developed to treat the human ailment, but they can be expensive. Why not try the same drugs on Max? If animals have emotions and can even develop similar emotional disturbances to humans, why not expect them to respond to the latest psychiatric medications like humans do?

We chose one of the less expensive of the anti-anxiety drugs, Mellaril, to try on Max. Scaling the dosage for a dog, we began treatments and within several weeks he showed marked improvement. He continued to improve over time and Max now leads a pretty normal life in western Washington. His owner is happy in spite of the $100 per month he has to shell out for the medication. I'm happy too, because my success with Max is pretty convincing evidence that animals do have emotions.

CHAPTER 8

We Seem to Be Having Some Technical Difficulties

The heart and soul of a good veterinary practice are its technicians. Veterinary technicians can fill the role that nurses fill in human medicine or if licensed (requiring two years of training) they can even fill a physician's assistant's role. A good technician will do preliminary physical exams, give injections, draw blood, take X rays, carry out all kinds of laboratory tests, provide instructions and advice to worried clients over the phone, even close superficial surgical incisions. In a busy practice, they are often expected to be working on half a dozen of these tasks at once, without getting confused and making mistakes. We ask a lot of our techs, in other words. But for someone whose job performance is so crucial and difficult, veterinary technicians are not particularly well-paid, which means that good ones are hard to keep. Good ones tend to move up and move on to better paying jobs. Quite a few even go on to vet school.

Not surprisingly, one of the qualities that make a good technician is how they relate to animals. They have to like and understand animals, not be afraid of them. Lack of fear is particularly important, because all techs must master the art of animal restraint.

Animals don't necessarily understand that the strange person who is trying to flex their injured ankle or pierce their neck with a long needle is really trying to help them. Humans even need reminding of this occasionally. I've always thought that the reason the doctor warns you, "This will just sting for a second," is so they don't get reflexively popped in the mouth from time to time.

But you can't verbally remind animals that their doctor is their friend, so in order that veterinarians don't get maimed or end up piercing an animal's eye with their hypodermic rather than a vein, someone, a tech, has to hold the animal while the needle is inserted. Proper restraint means immobilizing an animal in a position where the appropriate medical procedure can be done without its attacking or escaping. A frightened tech is liable to either under-restrain and get you bitten, or over-restrain, meaning injure or psychologically traumatize the animal. Animals have been killed in the vet's office from over-restraint by a frightened tech.

A tech working for me has it rough. He or she might have to restrain anything from a flying squirrel to an emu to a python. Therefore my techs need to recognize how they might inadvertently hurt an animal, how to prevent escape, and how to control the relevant weaponry. There are tricks which you develop with each species. Dogs are easy. You don't need tricks for them. Dogs have one weapon, their mouth. Control the mouth and no one will get hurt. Even exceptionally vicious dogs are not much problem once they are muzzled. If a dog is vicious enough, I hand the muzzle to the owner. If an owner is too frightened of his own dog to muzzle it, then he needs to find a vet even crazier than I am.

Cats are a different story. They are quicker than dogs, plus they literally bristle with weapons. Cats can and will bite, but they don't have to. Their claws have been used to disembowel prey for millennia. If you forget this fact, a cat will soon remind you. I once read of a fur trapper in the Old West who one day happened upon a lynx sleeping on a log. Lynx fur was apparently valuable in those days, and not having a weapon with him at the time, he decided that as a burly macho trapper, he would tiptoe up to the lynx and grab it around the neck. For the rest of his life he was known by the nickname "Scars."

One easy way to handle small cats, particularly if you only need to deal with their head, is to wrap them in a thick towel with the head just sticking out a bit. This neutralizes four of their five weapons and you just need to avoid the teeth. This is also a pretty good technique for other animals with several weapons like iguanas, which besides teeth have a spiny tail with which to swat you. The technique has limited use for larger cats. A cougar swathed in a towel can still be a bit of a problem.

With birds, the big problem is preventing escape. You can't just grab a leg because their legs are easily broken. If you do hold the legs, you have to hold both of them, and clasp them firmly as close to the body as possible. The easiest thing for restraining birds is some sort of straitjacket.

For small birds, the cardboard cylinder inside toilet paper rolls works nicely. For somewhat larger birds up to the size of parrots, segments of pantyhose make nice straitjackets. Slitting a small hole in the side of the pantyhose allows you to extract a wing or a leg, for instance, so you can draw blood from a wing vein or a toe.

Larger birds you don't have to worry so much about injuring. You have to worry about them injuring you. Herons and egrets, for instance, can be very dangerous if you are not used to handling them. They use their sword-like beaks not to bite but to spear and they can strike with all the speed and considerably more power than most snakes. The best thing to do with an injured egret is to immediately impale a large cork on the end of its beak. You might still get a black eye if you're not careful, but at least you will have an eye. Birds of prey also can be tricky. Their beaks look intimidating, but their beaks are not their weapons, their talons are. The key to handling birds of prey is avoiding the talons. Larger birds are even easier. I handle an emu by putting a hood over its head and sitting on it.

Vet techs, at least the ones who work for me, have to know all this about animal restraint and more. They also have to master, and be able to juggle, a variety of clinical tasks. Of course, my most memorable experiences with techs have not been with the ones who were perfect, never erred, could remember what needed done in eight separate cases before I thought to tell them. They made my life uneventfully pleasant. No, my most memorable experiences have been with those techs who were missing one or more of the key ingredients necessary to do the job well. They weren't bad or negligent people, necessarily. Usually they were good people trying to do their job as best they could. They just weren't cut out for the job.

Without question, my most memorable tech was Erin. Erin wasn't hired, she was inherited. I had just joined a practice with a new owner in a small Boston suburb. We hired one new tech, Sherry, to train from scratch. Sherry may have been untrained, but she was very bright. Then in her mid-thirties, Sherry had been married with a child by the time she was sixteen, and had never before had a chance to develop her considerable talents for working with animals. She turned out to be one of the better techs I have ever worked with and is still in the business today.

Erin was not new to working with vets. She had worked for years as a tech for the former owner of the clinic, and Dr. L., my new boss, saw no reason not to keep her on. She was very sweet and the clients of the former owner adored her for her easy sympathy and sunny disposition. She also loved animals and did a fine job restraining them. She wasn't highly trained because the previous doctor apparently didn't believe in medicine as practiced after 1950, but she was upbeat and eager to learn. I was particularly fond of her because in addition to being easy to work with she also taught me the Boston Law of the Conservation of "Rs." That law is that any "Rs" dropped from some words have to reappear in others. So as we reorganized the exam rooms, Erin labeled the drawers "Syringe Draw," "Bandage Draw," "Blood Tube Draw" and so on, just like she said it. These "Rs" reappeared whenever we had an animal with an upset stomach. Erin also wrote medical records with phonetic precision. They were having frequent "varmiting."

If Dr. L. had even the slightest thought about letting her go when he purchased the practice, Erin's personal situation made it all but impossible for anyone but a cad. Her mother, with whom she lived alone, had died unexpectedly just a few months previously. Erin didn't mope, though. She kept her smile all the while, and worked even harder at learning the new duties we were trying to teach her.

Despite her endearing human qualities, I suspected Erin wasn't going to work out as a technician in our new, very successful, and therefore increasingly hectic clinic even before the day she mistakenly cut the ears off Rascal Roeder. Her problem was that when things got too busy, she got flustered. When she got flustered, she tended to lose track of what she was doing in the here and now and worry about future problems. I first noticed this when she interrupted me one day in the middle of an appointment to ask if cats under anesthesia usually passed a lot of gas. Passed a lot of gas? I excused myself and headed for the operating room. This was worrisome.

The OR indeed reeked of passed intestinal gas. There was also the appropriate, familiar, and utterly characteristic sound of passing gas, only it was continuous like an exhalation that never ended, or like someone had sat on the world's largest pooh-pooh cushion. There was no one in the room but me and the cat, and I knew the sound wasn't coming from me. What could be going on?

For major surgery, we usually put animals under with an injection, and keep them under during the operation with an anesthetic gas administered either through a mask or a tube inserted directly down the trachea into the lungs. For minor surgery, though, we will often "box down" a cat. That is, skip the injection (which takes a while to wear off even after the surgery) and put them in what amounts to sealed fish tank—a clear plastic box with a mixture of oxygen and anesthesia running in through a tube at one end and out a separate tube at the other. After they fall peacefully to sleep, we take them out of the box and continue anesthesia through a mask.

The key to using this technique successfully is remembering to turn a valve on the gas anesthesia machine when you switch from the box to the mask. This valve switches the machine from continuous gas flow, which you need for the box, to a mode which allows an animal to exhale. In this mode when back-pressure from the expanding lungs reaches a threshold, the machine temporarily interrupts the gas flow, allowing the animal to exhale back into the mask and out a separate tube. I'd never thought about it before, but as I looked at the cat on the table I realized that if you forgot to turn this valve, you could blow up an animal like you would blow up a balloon with a bottle of compressed air.

Indeed, the cat looked like a overfilled balloon. It was much too spherical for a cat, and its legs stuck out stiffly as if it had fallen and was bracing for the impact. Luckily, unlike a balloon filling from a compressed air machine, animals have at least one other way for gas to escape. This cat's lungs had filled as far as they could fill, and the back-pressure was diverting the gas down the esophagus, through the stomach and intestines and out the other end. The surgical drape over the hindquarters billowed gently in the breeze.

We were lucky. The cat wasn't injured. The gas mixture had had plenty of oxygen at the time so it hadn't suffocated. Also, we were using a mask rather than a "trach" tube, as we call it. With the mask, gas could easily leak over into the digestive system. With a "trach" tube, direct gas pressure to the lungs would have been much higher and they might have ruptured and killed the cat. After adjusting the machine, I performed the minor surgery without further incident. But this was the sort of error that was unacceptable and could have turned out much worse. Strike one, I thought to myself.

Things were also plenty busy the afternoon Ron Roeder hauled his two coon hounds, Rascal and Buck, through the front door and let them bleed all over the waiting room. The receptionist paged me immediately, because it looked to her as if the dogs might bleed to death at any moment.

Roeder was a local farmer, a gruff New Englander with a not-so-well-disguised soft spot for animals. The dogs, which were usually buddies, were kept together in his barn. They had got into a squabble over a bitch in heat. They weren't badly injured, but had managed to chew a few holes in each other's ears. Coon hounds have those long floppy ears and ear wounds can bleed a lot, so it looked like they were hurt much worse than they actually were. I had much more serious cases I needed to deal with first, so I flopped both their ears over the top of their heads and ran a bandage snugly around the head in order to hold the ears in place and control their bleeding. I told Roeder to come back in the morning. It looked like they would both need some stitches.

That turned out to be an understatement. Later in the evening, when we were mopping up on treatments that we hadn't time to do during business hours, I asked Erin to get Rascal. By now, I always made sure I administered the anesthesia. Once he was safely and stably asleep, I turned to another case, asking Erin to cut off his bandage so we could assess the damage.

"He's still bleeding a lot, Dr. K," Erin said with effort as she worked hard to cut through his bandage with surgical scissors.

I looked at Rascal's ears. Once. Then again. And again. "Erin," I stammered in disbelief, "you just...you just cut off his ears!"

Erin didn't believe me until I picked the bandage up off the floor and peeled the ends of his ears off it to show her. She was upset, needless to say, and so was I. I sent her home for the night and took care of Roeder's other dog by myself. The only one who didn't seem particularly upset by the whole affair was Roeder himself, especially once he found out that there would be no charge for treating his animals. I had evened out Rascal's ear-remnants as best I could, and sutured the new ear margins. Rascal no longer had floppy coon hound ears. He didn't have the perky ears of a cropped Doberman either. His ears stood up a bit, pointed out a bit. Actually, they now looked something like helicopter propellers. "What the hell'd he need those long ears for anyway?" growled Rocder when he picked him up. "He's just a barn dog." But I was still brooding about Erin's mistake. Strike two, I thought.

Strike three was the insulin overdose. I only found out about it by accident when our tech-in-training, Sherry, poked her head in the door to ask me in a concerned voice if the insulin dose for a diabetic cat should nearly fill a hypodermic syringe. Of course not, I replied, why? Earlier during routine treatment, she had seen Erin inject a syringeful of insulin into Rex, a diabetic cat that we were boarding. She'd been thinking about it and was concerned because she thought she remembered that when I gave an insulin injection, it was only a fraction of that amount. Dropping everything, I sprinted for the kennels where I found Rex glassy-eyed and stumbling around like a punch-drunk boxer.

Wanting to be sure what his problem was, I sent someone looking for Erin while I pricked his ear and took a quick blood sugar reading. Insulin is a hormone that allows glucose, the form of sugar in the blood, to be transported from the blood itself into the surrounding tissues where it can be broken down to provide the body's energy. Too little insulin keeps glucose in the blood and out of the tissues, causing all sorts of health problems. That's why people and animals that can't make enough insulin on their own need to get injections daily, or even more often. Too much insulin, on the other hand, drives too much glucose out of the blood, so that tissues like the brain which have a high and continuous need for it, begin to starve. Deprived even briefly of glucose, the brain, in fact, takes a vacation. Lights out. Coma can be nearly immediate, with death not far behind, unless the glucose supply is restored.

Rex's glucose was low all right—really low. I grabbed a jar of Karo syrup and smeared some on his gums. Karo contains a lot of glucose. It enters the blood stream directly without having to be processed and is useful stuff to have on hand when there's a diabetic in the family. In fact, I tell people with diabetic animals to keep a jar around, just in case. I was glad I had taken my own advice. Just then Erin walked in.

"Erin!" I'm afraid I shouted. "What the hell happened? You didn't really give him that whole syringe, did you?"

"I gave him whatever you wrote down," she wailed, clearly upset herself, "That's all."

Then I understood what had happened. I had written 5.0 units on my treatment instructions, and she had misread the decimal point on a 50 unit syringe. Twice the normal insulin dose was serious. Rex had gotten ten times his usual dose.

I rubbed more syrup on his gums and put him on an IV dextrose drip. He was too far out of it to protest. Like most diabetics, Rex got injections of a slow-acting insulin preparation, so its effects would be spread out over most of a day. That was lucky. He might be comatose for a few hours, but I knew with treatment we would pull him through. I couldn't help thinking, though, what if Sherry hadn't said anything to me and I had gone home for the night? Left untreated, Rex would have been a goner by morning. We couldn't continue to have these fiascoes. My nerves weren't up to it.

Erin had to go. As fond as Dr. L. and I were of her personally, we were ready to fire her. She certainly did get along well with our clients though and was still an exceptionally sweet person. She was just a miserable technician. If we could keep her away from the animals, she was great to have around. Dr. L and I put our heads together. We decided that the personal qualities Erin possessed in abundance would make her an ideal receptionist.

And a fine receptionist she turned out to be. Clients were happy to see her. She made pleasant chit-chat with them as they sat in the waiting room. She did get appointment times mixed up occasionally, but we could live with those mistakes. Otherwise she worked out fine.

A year or so later, when we were both able to joke about it, I asked Erin whatever could have made her think she could give a cat so much insulin. "I think I got it mixed up with the human dose," she offered.

"Human dose? What do you mean?" I was confused now.

"Oh, I forgot you weren't here yet. Just before my mom died, they found out she was diabetic. I had to give her insulin shots every day. They didn't seem to do her any good, though. She died not long after."

I thought it best not to say what I was thinking.

CHAPTER 9

A Bird in the Hand

I was just about to enter the bird ward one cold December evening to check on a couple of my patients—an owl and a bald cockatoo, as I recall—when some moaning coming from the other side of the door stopped me in my tracks, my hand literally on the doorknob. A woman's voice pleaded urgently, "Oh God, yes! Yes! Faster! Don't stop! Please don't stop!"

I certainly didn't want to walk in on that. I was a senior vet student at the time and it sounded like a couple of the other vet students were having it off in the bird ward. Vet students are, after all, healthy vigorous young people, so I wasn't too surprised. Even the location wasn't particularly surprising. Our bird ward was a converted locker room, spacious enough to find plenty of places to lie down. Senior students even slept there occasionally when they were on call. Maybe the students inside right now, whoever they were, would be sleeping soon too. I decided I could just as easily return a bit later to check on my patients.

Bird medicine had attracted me for nearly as long as I had wanted to be a veterinarian. But medicine for pet birds didn't exist to any real extent before I went to vet school in the early 1980s. There was poultry medicine, but that was a different culture altogether. Treating animals raised for commercial purposes, where cost is the only consideration, is always very foreign to the pet treatment culture. Vets who forget this can end up in trouble. As one example, the typical way you treat a diseased poultry flock is to select one bird from the flock, kill it, and try to figure out from a postmortem exam what was wrong with it. You then use that information to work out a treatment plan for the rest of the flock.

When I was an undergraduate in Indiana, working as a veterinary technician at a local clinic, I remember quite clearly a pleasant young couple bringing in their pet chicken because it had developed a sneeze and cough. The vet I worked for at the time was from the old school of doctors. He knew what he knew, he did what he did, and expected no one to question him about it. He was also not the most sensitive person in the world to the needs and desires of others. In this particular case, he couldn't quite get his mind around the concept of someone having a chicken for a pet. So, he acted as he would have with any poultry farmer. He told the couple to come back the next day, he would look into the problem. Then he took the bird in back, killed it, autopsied it, and sure enough discovered why it was sneezing and coughing. Quite pleased with his success, he cheerfully tried to explain the disease to the horrified couple the next morning when they came to pick up their bird and was irritated that they weren't eager to listen.

Apparently I wasn't the only one in those days who thought that pet birds should get more medical attention.

Several years before I entered vet school, some of Cornell's students had organized their own program in bird medicine. The school had allowed them to turn the old locker room into a bird ward, and senior students were in charge of treating whatever birds were brought in, asking for help from the teaching faculty when they thought it might be useful. The student program ran along strict hierarchical lines depending on seniority. As a freshman, you were expected to do the mindless drudgery—cleaning cages, feeding, and watering all the patients daily. But as you progressed from year to year through school, you gradually assumed more and more responsibility, being taught by older students. By senior year, you were handling cases on your own, sometimes even doing your own orthopedic surgery, and helping to train the underclassman. By the time I was a senior, almost all nonpoultry bird medicine had become wildlife rehabilitation, trying to fix up various hawks or owls that had been shot, poisoned, or hit by cars, rather than treating pets. But you could learn a lot about birds doing wildlife rehabilitation.

Today, I often tell my students that an animal is an animal is an animal. In other words, that the same medical principles should be applied no matter what species you are treating. This is true in a certain sense. But also in another very practical sense, it still helps to have experience with the particular species you are working on. Years ago, I watched a very conscientious orthopedic surgeon blow a lovely pet macaw to pieces while trying to repair its broken wing, because he had no experience with birds.

To understand what happened, you need to know that birds have a very different kind of respiratory system than we do. Their system is actually much better. A superior respiratory system, in fact, is one thing that allows birds such spectacular feats of endurance as flying nonstop for three days and nights while migrating from Alaska to Fiji.

Humans respire by pumping air in and out of the same chamber, our lungs, like a bellows. Because we can't evacuate all the used air from our lungs even when exhaling to the fullest, our lungs can at best contain a mixture of fresh air that we just inhaled and oxygen-depleted air we couldn't exhale. By contrast, birds have a series of tubes and air sacs that allow them to circulate fresh air continuously through their lungs. Amazingly, they breathe pure fresh air both when they exhale and inhale.

Another thing that helps birds fly is that their long wing and leg bones are hollow, filled with air instead of marrow like ours, making them very light. Most birds' skeletons actually weigh less than their feathers. The upper wing bone of birds, equivalent to our humerus or upper arm bone, has what in this case was a fatal peculiarity. Its hollow interior is connected directly to an air sac. Birds breathe into their upper arms, in other words.

This poor, unsuspecting orthopedic surgeon didn't realize that the mixture of oxygen and anesthesia gas the macaw was breathing through its treacheal tube was leaking out the end of the broken humerus into the wing tissue, even as he was using an electric cauterizer to seal off some small blood vessels. Birds, compared to dogs or cats, are small, which means they don't have much blood. You have to be very careful to minimize blood loss during surgery. I can only guess that the cauterizer must have sparked, but there was a sudden flash and a loud pop, and the operating room suddenly had feathers, flesh, and smoke wafting through it. The patient was in pieces. Today we have better cauterizers, and safer anesthesia gases, so this type of accident probably couldn't occur anymore, thank God.

Having seen, even before getting to vet school, some of the misadventures that naive veterinarians could have treating birds, plus having my own four years of experience while in vet school, by the time I was a senior I felt I knew most of the unexpected curves that bird patients could throw you. Of course, I was thinking of medical issues. I was confident that I had them under control. On this particular night, I knew that my owl's broken wing was healing nicely, and I thought I had the baldness of the cockatoo figured out too. Returning to the bird ward very late, I found everything quiet. The extracurricular activities seemed to be finished for the evening. I tiptoed into the darkened ward to see if I could check on my patients without waking them.

The cockatoo seemed to be sleeping peacefully. I was peering into the owl's cage, when from behind me came the same moaning insistent voice. "Oh God, yes! Yes! Faster! Don't stop! Please don't stop!" I almost dropped, whether from fright or embarrassment I'm not sure. Spinning around to apologize for intruding, there was no one to be seen. The cockatoo was now wide awake though. He blinked at me. "Oh God, yes! Yes! Faster! Don't stop! Please don't stop!" he said in a plaintive woman's voice.

No one really understands why some bird species are such good mimics. Indeed, most people don't even realize how good some species can be. They think that croaking "Polly want a cracker" like in old television shows is as good as birds can do. Not hardly. I have a pet now, an African gray parrot named Googly, who imitates our phone so well he always has someone sprinting to answer a phantom ring. If we ignore him, he continues on and does our answering machine, the recorded voice plus the various clicks, beeps, and hums. He can also do the vacuum cleaner, dog fights, children yelling at one another, parents yelling at children. It can be pretty embarrassing when we have company. I remember another parrot that did a perfect rendition of all its owner's kitchen appliances, the toaster, the blender, and the microwave, even the appropriate beeps as it turned off.

My introduction to the creative use of bird mimicry came during that same year from one of Cornell's retired English professors. He was the perfect stereotype of an English professor, complete with elaborately curled white mustache, tweed hat, tweed jacket with patches at the elbows, an air of abstraction, and a suite of cultivated eccentricities. I wasn't sure whether keeping pet cockroaches was one of these eccentricities, but I'll never forget the enormous cockroach that crawled out of one of his jacket pockets as he was explaining his pet mynah bird's problem to me.

"I've been frightfully upset by this recent lump on her breast..." He was saying something like this as, transfixed, I watched the cockroach crawl up his lapel, around the back of his mufflered neck, down the other lapel, and into his other jacket pocket. As soon as it disappeared, I tuned back in. "...hoping it's not serious. You do have experience with mynah birds, I trust? They're related to starlings, you know."

I examined the lump. A small tumor, all right. It would have to be surgically removed. We would both keep our fingers crossed that it wasn't malignant.

We scheduled the surgery for the next day. Mr. Chips, as I had begun thinking of him, was exceptionally nervous. Nervous enough that I felt obligated to talk one of our clinical surgeons into doing the procedure, even though I felt confident I could do it as well myself. Some people when nervous rattle on about whatever pops into their mind. This is what Mr. Chips did. He told me the whole story of why he had got the bird. It was because he was a bit frightened living alone in a large house. He wanted canine home protection, but the fact that he was frightened of dogs complicated things. He decided to buy a good bird mimic, and solve his home protection problem by training it to bark like a large guard dog. Right after he got it, he left the bird with a friend who owned a very vocal German shepherd. After a couple of weeks the bird indeed did a series of German shepherd barks and growls that were indistinguishable from the real thing. Fortunately for Mr. Chips, the tumor was benign, the bird recovered without complications, so all his inventive efforts had not gone for naught.

In reality, Mr. Chips was fortunate in another sense too. Birds don't always mimic the sounds you want them to imitate. They have minds of their own after all. In the small hospital in the Boston area where I used to work, we once boarded a pet parrot that had been taught with great effort and patience to imitate the sounds of barnyard animals. The bird did perfect pigs, cows, and horses. It did a good rooster too. I guess the owner liked to imagine that instead of living in suburban Boston he lived on a farm in the country. Maybe he even visited a farm on his vacation. If so, he should have taken his parrot. During the two weeks in our clinic while the owner was vacationing, it learned to do a variety of maniacally barking and howling dog sounds. Of course, the parrot much preferred doing barking dogs to doing farm animals. The owner was furious, but I don't know what he expected.

I'm sure that my bald cockatoo's owners did not expect him to pick up the vocalizations that he did either. The bird's medical problem was what I now would recognize in an instant as psittacine-beak-and-feather disease, a viral infection that destroys feathers, but more importantly destroys some of the cells of the immune system. However, at that time the virus had not been identified and I wasn't sure what the problem was. It can be behavioral. Some birds pluck out their own feathers when they are nervous.

The owners had brought the bird from their home in a suburb of New York City, more than three hours away by car, and because of their work schedule could not return to pick it up until the following weekend. In the meantime, word about the sounds made by the bald cockatoo spread through the clinic. I must admit some culpability here. It was too priceless not to let other students in on. A crowd of students and doctors began to reliably cluster around the door of the bird ward at lights-out, when the cockatoo liked to begin its performance. I was pumped for every detail that I could recall about the owners. But I really could recall almost nothing about them. I had been concentrated on the bird during their visit. "What are you going to say to them?" people wanted to know. I didn't plan to say anything. This poor couple probably already had enough trouble when their parents or Aunt Bessie came for a visit.

On the day they were scheduled to pick up their cockatoo, I noticed that the clinic was exceptionally full of medical personnel. Vet students meandered here and there, pretending to be busy. There were even a suspiciously large number of doctors about, working on their records. I wonder now if the couple, who turned out to be an exceptionally handsome pair, and may have been actors or models, felt any special attention while they sat in the waiting room.

In the exam room, I explained their bird's problem. Alas, there was little we could do. Viral infections were difficult. The bird might die in a month or live ten years, we couldn't be sure. Then before I could stop it, out of my mouth popped, "By the way, where in the house do you keep your bird?"

"Where? You mean what room? The bedroom, why?" They looked at each other. The woman turned as red as a tomato. "Oh, no. He didn't really, did he?" she said without much hope.

"I'm afraid he did," I replied. Now embarrassed myself, I hoped that as they left I wouldn't hear the waiting room break into wild applause.

CHAPTER 10

Monty—Psycho-python

Real people don't own snakes either. Harold, a one-time field assistant for my zoologist husband, is a perfect example.

Harold Ripner, "The Rip" as he like to be called, had three passions in life, snakes, guns, and television, probably in that order. To understand Harold, you had to see where he lived—a large dilapidated house trailer on the edge of a small town on the hot and humid plains of South Carolina. The living room of his trailer was the closest thing to an indoor landfill I've seen—or smelled. Except for a sheet-covered couch in one corner connected by narrow footpaths to the television and refrigerator, there was no part of his living room that wasn't crammed with overflowing garbage cans. From the aroma, I guessed they contained a lot of old food, some soiled newspapers, coffee grounds, half-empty beer bottles, and at least several years worth of ashtray dumpings. Maybe, though, I was only smelling the sticky residue of what had leaked out on to the floor.

The smell of rotting garbage of course attracts flies, which Harold didn't mind, because he liked to entertain guests by catching flies, tearing off their wings, and using them to entice his pet lizards out from among the garbage cans. Harold was partial to geckos, those wall-climbing tropical lizards, although he was never sure how many actually lived with him at any one time.

Most snake owners keep their animals in cages or glass terraria. Not Harold. He had converted one whole bedroom into free-range snake habitat. The snake room (or seventh circle as I mentally referred to it) had no furniture, just a few dead tree branches tangled into a snake jungle gym. Large plastic tarps covered the floor, presumably as some sort of disposable cage liner. Snakes like heat, so heat lamps also hung from the walls and ceiling. Stepping into the room in the summer was kind of like stepping into the muggy tropics.

If you feared snakes, on the other hand, or even if they made you just a bit edgy, stepping into the room was more like stepping into your worst nightmare. Because in the room snakes roamed freely—dozens of snakes. Small skinny ones, large fat ones, and all sorts in between, slithering across the tarp, coiled around the jungle-gym or each other, sometimes just basking happily beneath the heat lamps. And because Harold generally went into the room only when he fed or played with them, the snakes were trained to expect a little entertainment or perhaps tasty morsels of still-twitching rats or mice from any humans they saw. They rapidly converged on any human visitor, crawling over and on to them. This can be disconcerting even if you don't mind snakes.

The only animal I didn't much like in that room was

Harold's python, and that was only because it didn't seem to want to accept with good grace the fact that I had no food for it. When Harold tried to remove it from my leg, it immediately bit him, leaving comb-like rows of blood droplets on his forearm. But snake owners don't mind bites. It comes with the territory. This python was about eight feet long, and bit Harold pretty often.

People rarely get killed by their pet snakes, but it's possible if the snake is very big and the owner does something very stupid. Snakes don't eat people, or even try to eat people. We're too big. In order to get killed by your snake you have to work at it. But it has happened.

Pythons, like other constrictors, kill their prey by striking with blinding speed, seizing the prey's head while throwing several body coils around it, and squeezing it until it suffocates. Only then do they start swallowing it whole in that endearing snake manner.

One of the few snake owners to be killed recently by his pet python forgot about this scenario apparently. Rats reared to be pets, laboratory animals, or snake food have been bred to be docile when handled. You can do nearly anything you want to them unless it is painful. They stay relaxed even when dangled in odd physical positions, making them a veterinarian's delight. This unfortunate fellow tucked the rat he intended to feed his snake under his chin, so he could use both hands to open the door in the top of his python's cage. The snake did what snakes do. It rocketed through the open door striking the rat, at the same time threw several quick coils around its owner's neck, thus bringing down a much larger prey than it expected.

Harold told me the story, which I think may have haunted him. He lived alone, so there was no one to help him if he got in trouble with the python. From his attitude, my guess is that he had had at least one near-miss. Normal people might react to this sort of fright by getting rid of the snake, or confining it to a cage into which its food could be thrown. But Harold instead taped capsules of amyl nitrite in assorted locations around the walls of the snake room. Amyl nitrite capsules, if broken open under a snake's nostrils by a still conscious snake owner in trouble, reputedly make them uncoil, although Harold had not had yet put this theory to test when we knew him.

Snake fanciers like other eccentrics often lose perspective. I once asked Harold, proud owner of this smelly, squalid, snake-strewn trailer, why he kept so many pistols in his house. "Home protection," he murmured solemnly.

So if I knew some of the problems, and even dangers, of owning a very large snake, and normal people don't own snakes anyway, how did we end up with Monty, the psycho-python from hell?

The short answer is that I hate to euthanize animals except for medically compelling reasons. Some people will put animals down at the drop of a hat. For instance, I have had a request to euthanize a pet because the owner's house had been redecorated and the pet was no longer color-coordinated with the upholstery. When I refuse these requests, I try to come up with an alternative way to dispose of the animal, such as finding another home for it. Otherwise the owner will just take it to a less squeamish veterinarian.

Monty, a ten-foot-long reticulated python, was brought in to be euthanized because he had bitten his owner pretty seriously. The owner, with one heavily bandaged hand, turned out to be a notorious local drug dealer, and Monty had very obviously had an abused childhood.

Most pet pythons like to be handled. They particularly like coiling around your body for the warmth. But not Monty. Monty hated people. Even the sight of someone walking past his cage was enough to make him strike. Consequently his nose was always beat up from bashing into the glass cage window.

"What if I take him home instead? Would that be okay with you?" It popped out of my mouth before I even knew it was coming. I've always been a sucker for abused animals. *There are really no bad animals, only mistreated ones* has always been my philosophy.

Monty's owner looked at me with disbelief, then with wicked amusement. "Be my guest," he chuckled.

My husband, Steve, was not amused by the coffin-sized cage containing a petulant python that appeared in the living room. Always more practical about these things than I am, the first thing he did was add several more locks to the cage door.

A ten-foot python could easily kill a pet or a person, if the situation were right. We didn't want to lose any dogs or cats to Monty. He then asked reasonably, "How will we even clean the cage?" A good point. Unless we wanted our home smelling like Harold's before long, we would have to clean the cage of snake droppings and shed skin from time to time.

We finally worked out a method. Timing was critical. We always cleaned the cage a couple of days after Monty ate, when he was still digesting his nice meal of rats. At that point, he was as satisfied and sedate as he would ever be. Steve would quietly open the cage top, grab Monty just behind the head so that he couldn't be bitten, and haul his wildly thrashing body out of the cage. Monty didn't like this anymore than we did, so he did everything in his power to make it more trouble than it was worth, including crapping frantically and copiously and voiding his foul-smelling anal glands on the person handling him. Eventually Steve began stripping down to shorts for this chore. That way, he only had to shower and wash one pair of shorts in order to no longer smell like python anal glands.

With Monty out of the cage, the real fun began. Steve would hold Monty's head with both hands while being jerked and flung around the room like he was wrestling a high pressure fire hose. In the meantime, I'd begin cleaning Monty's cage like crazy. I'd have to stop whenever Steve yelled because that meant that Monty had managed to flip a coil around some vital part of his anatomy. Usually, it was just his arms. Monty could quickly cut off the circulation and his arms would begin going numb. Continuing to hold on to a large irate python can be difficult if you can't feel your fingers.

It isn't all that hard to uncoil a snake, even a large one, if you begin at the tail. Of course, first you have to *find* the tail. But once you do so, it's pretty routine. So I would free Steve's arms as quickly as I could, and return to my cleaning. It only usually took two or three cycles of these cleaning-uncoiling bouts and we were done. Monty would be stuffed back into his cage until the next time, a few weeks later.

Like I say, snake owners tend to lose perspective. In fact, we never really realized what lunacy our lives had slipped into because of Monty until we had a visit from some friends we hadn't seen for years. These were old, dear college chums who had known us before we had a house full of strange animals. They probably already realized we were a little...unusual. But they could hardly have been prepared for the sight that greeted them when after ringing the doorbell, I yelled, "It's open."

They hadn't chosen the best time for a visit. Monty had developed pneumonia. Snakes, with their long skinny lungs, are prone to pneumonia. This meant that we had to haul him out of his cage every other day for treatment, instead of every few weeks for cage cleaning. The treatment consisted of injections of antibiotics and large amounts of fluids were needed to flush the antibiotics through his system. Since you can't simply order an obstreperous python to drink more water, we had to inject the fluids under his skin.

To understand the problem this presented with Monty, imagine your doctor trying to give you a subcutaneous injection of several ounces of fluid just after you discovered a bumblebee buzzing around inside your pants. But we had developed a technique for doing this. The key was speed. Use the biggest needle on the largest possible syringe. While Monty twisted and Steve lurched around, I tried to grab some part of the snake—any part of the snake. With one hand, I would jam the needle under the skin. With the other hand, drive the plunger home as quickly as possible. It took a lot of tries to give Monty all his fluids. Often, the needle would come loose from Monty and from the syringe, occasionally speeding across the room like a blow dart because of the pressure I'd put on it.

Alas, our friends had arrived when we were in the midst of this fiasco. We hadn't seen them for a few years and I don't think they even knew we had a snake. Like most of our good friends, they knocked and walked right on in. What greeted them was Steve, in his shorts, staggering around the living room with a humongous python coiled around him. I was trying to stab the snake with the biggest hypodermic they had probably ever seen and we were yelling rather breathlessly at each other.

"Hold him still, forchristsakes."

"What do you think I'm trying to do? Do you have anything in him yet?"

"Dammit, missed again."

"Oh, oh, my hands are numb. Find the tail. Hurry!"

There was no time to explain, of course. I finally got one syringeful into him, fumbled for a second syringe, and drove it home too. We aimed Monty's head in the general direction of the cage door and managed to stuff him back in his home sweet home.

It took a while to catch my breath. Steve sat inertly on the floor too exhausted to say anything. He waved weakly toward the door. Oh yes, our friends. Time to be a hostess. I turned to give them an official, if belated, hello, but they were gone. The front door swung wide open. They must have left at a run. An hour or so later Tim, the husband, called to apologize. "It looked like you were going to be busy for a while. We didn't want to interrupt you, and we couldn't stay that long, anyway. Also Laurie, maybe you didn't know, doesn't like snakes. Even garter snakes. We decided to stay at a motel."

I guess they just didn't understand what a special greeting they had received.

CHAPTER 11

Just Think If He'd Really Been Sick

I've always been certain that people can learn a lot from pets. Kyle, my twelve-year-old terrorist houseguest, certainly did. Kyle came for a weeklong visit and left a calmer and much wiser boy, especially about how to behave when visiting Auntie Veronika.

The son of a dear friend, Kyle had grown up in emotional turmoil involving the progressive psychological deterioration of his mother. While a good kid some of the time, at other times he exhibited some behaviors you could live without. For one thing, he had his own special brand of state-of-the art tantrums, involving glass-shattering shrieks and blizzards of shrapnel from random, breakable objects. Even as a toddler, one of these tantrums was sufficiently impressive that it could empty out a quiet restaurant quicker than a bomb threat. If nothing breakable was within reach, he improvised. Once, when he was nine, I watched him improvise a surprisingly powerful and accurate roundhouse to his father's testicles. So far as I knew, he had never actually tried to burn down a house during a tantrum, but I never put it past him either. Kyle, in other words, could be a challenging houseguest.

Even without houseguests who detonate at unexpected moments, life can be difficult for a veterinarian's pet. You're likely to be a guinea pig for the latest vaccines or diets, and maybe an involuntary blood donor if one is needed. Now that I teach veterinary students, my pets must also suffer the unpracticed pokes, prods, and punctures that veterinarians-in-training must learn to do well.

Annie, my elderly, blind, three-legged terrier, is called on particularly often as a teaching aide. A wayward car took Annie's leg when she was a pup. Old age took her eyesight. But nothing has taken her enthusiasm for life. Despite her ailments, Annie still gets thrilled about an extra food treat or a casual caress. What makes her so useful as a teaching tool is that, as has happened, if a student performs a physical exam on her without noticing that she is one limb short of a quartet, or blind as true love, it gives me (and the student) a pretty good indication that he should probably pursue another line of work.

It was from another of my dogs, Wart, that Kyle learned his lesson though.

Wart was maybe my favorite dog of all time. A black Labrador, named not after the skin lesion but after King Arthur's nickname in T.H. White's *Once and Future King*, Wart's demeanor was anything but regal. He was a creature of mindless and indiscriminate loving enthusiasm, friendly to a crotch-nuzzling fault, living in the eternal now. For Wart, the world was always and ever a joyful place and everyone was his pal. We used to joke about how burglars had better beware of our house, because if they broke in when we were gone, Wart was very likely to lick them to death.

Having Kyle around was particularly joyful for Wart. Kyle loved Wart. And since Wart loved everyone, this was a nice match. He particularly loved anyone who would play with him every waking hour and sleep with him all night. Whenever Kyle visited, they would curl up together and sleep the sleep of the blessed. Wart was Kyle's Ritalin.

When Wart was with him, you could leave Kyle alone with Tiffany crystal, with your collection of Ming porcelain, with your grandmother's jewelry. Sometimes I wanted to leave him alone with our ten-foot psycho-python Monty, but my husband, Steve, vetoed that idea.

But their inseparability became something of a problem during one visit. Wart developed a touch of diarrhea, and I was afraid that their sleeping together might have some messy consequences. I also worried that Wart might pass on to Kyle whatever bacteria were causing his diarrhea, and the thought of dealing with an intestinally impaired Kyle was too horrible for serious consideration. So I took Wart to the hospital with me one morning to check out what might be causing his bowel problem in the first place. Kyle would have to go cold turkey for the day.

A lot of dogs are terrified of the hospital. After all, they don't usually go there for fun. Wart's terror took the form of a hyperactive eagerness to please. His tail beat faster, he nuzzled and licked anything in sight, and he worriedly followed me everywhere.

This particular day, I was hit with even more than the standard number of demands, requests, and emergencies as I walked in the hospital door. I even forgot that Wart was with me until heading into our pharmacy with its heavy swinging door, I heard a sharp yelp at my back. It never occurred to me that Wart might try to push his way through the door. In fact, it never occurred to me that he *could* push his way through such a heavy door. Swinging doors, in any case, are not designed for creatures with tails, and this one had swung shut on his tail. Of course, his immediate response after yelping was to nuzzle and lick everyone in sight even more frantically than before.

I couldn't deal with this continuing distraction to top of everything else, so I asked a tech to put him in any empty kennel, where he might stay out of trouble until I found time to look into his intestinal problem. Before long though, someone yelled from the kennel area, "Does anyone know the dog that's bleeding all over back here?"

It was Wart, of course. He was lying quietly in a small puddle of blood until he saw me, whereon he leapt to his feet, and with tail whipping frantically, sprayed blood like a lawn sprinkler nice and evenly all over me and the walls of the kennel. Drat. I would have to anesthetize him. There was no way I could examine his tail when he was so excited.

The tail turned out to be badly lacerated, probably broken. In either case, the treatment was the same, so I never bothered with X rays. Shave it, suture the wound, bandage it tightly enough to stabilize the area. While shaving his tail, my eyes drifted to Wart's testicles—one of which appeared to be much larger than the other. I felt it. Yep, it was true. One of his testicles was huge. This wasn't good.

There are lots of good reasons to neuter your pet. I go through the litany of reasons with my clients about this incessantly. One of the things I invariably mention is that neutered pets are less likely to get cancer. Cancer is a major killer, probably *the* major killer, of dogs. However, cancer of the reproductive organs (particularly testicular and prostate cancer in males, mammary and uterine cancer in females) can be virtually eliminated if the animals are neutered before adulthood. Testicular tumors are not usually malignant in dogs, but if they happen to be, the animal is invariably a goner. I was worried.

The prudent thing to do was something I should have done long ago—castrate him. I had vague hopes of breeding him, though, altruistically passing along those genes of pure love and joy. But that wasn't to be. In less than five minutes, his balls were in a bottle, waiting to be shipped to the pathologist. Castration is a surgery at which I'm exceptionally adept, as I occasionally remind Steve when he's done something particularly irritating. It's a trivial procedure, quick, painless, and easily done under the amount of anesthesia one might slip into, say, a morning cup of coffee.

When Wart awoke he appeared a bit confused.

Now where am I? My goodness, what's that huge scary white thing on my tail? Maybe it's eating my tail, cause it sure does hurt. And what's this? Oh my god. Where did they go? Maybe if I look around I can find them. Nope. Maybe I'm dreaming. I'm sure there were a couple of things down there this morning. Lordy, let me out of here. Maybe I can find them at home.

Well, I don't really know what he was thinking, but he was obviously very concerned. He sniffed, he licked, he licked and sniffed. He looked at me as if to say, "A touch of diarrhea, a trip to the office with your very best pal, the next thing you know your heavily bandaged tail aches like the blazes, and your are testicles gone. How could you do this to me?"

I felt pretty bad about things myself. I really had hoped to breed Wart, but obviously that opportunity had died. Later, it turned out that Wart's tumor was benign and he went on to live many more joyful years. However at the time, I was very worried. I was depressed and upset, and not ready to have to deal with Kyle during one of his bad spells. Maybe I could make lemonade from these lemons, though.

Arriving home, it was apparent that Kyle had missed Wart. He was bouncing around the house like a pinball in a pinball machine—flinging himself from one piece of furniture to another, shrieking like a Banshee. Lamps and chairs were overturned. The place looked as if it had been bombed. I was past being able to cope with this. Way past. As Kyle hurtled past, I grabbed him, cocked an eyebrow, gave him my most school-marmish, intimidating glare, and hissed, "Look, Kyle. Look at Wart." He looked uncertain and a little fearful, but then glanced at Wart's bandaged tail and the row of sutures where his scrotum once had been.

"What happened to poor Wartie?"

"I'll tell you what happened, Kyle. Poor Wartie got a little wild at the hospital. I was in a bad mood. A really bad mood like I'm in now. You interested in girls yet, Kyle? See what I did to him? It was all over in five minutes. Think about one other thing. Wart's my favorite." As I walked away, Kyle continued to stare at Wart, who now lay mournfully in the corner.

For the rest of his visit Kyle was an angel.

CHAPTER 12

Come On, Iggy, Say Hello to the Doctor

"Dr. K., could you please get up here? The iguana man is really out of control."

Of course he would be. Iguana owners are a special breed. You'd have to be to own a pet that looks like a pint-sized dinosaur with a bad hangover and the personality of a crowbar. I wondered what this particular iguanophile was doing to make my receptionist sound so desperate.

Iguana owners often have a special look as well—usually a sort of 1980s grunge with maybe with a faint overlay of whips-and-chains panache—torn T-shirts, heavy boots, elaborate tattoos, lots of black leather, spiked collars. Iguanas have spikes too—down their backs. Maybe there is some sort of spike-to-spike principle of attraction operating here. However at as much as five feet from head to tail, with formidable jaws, a glare that could turn a werewolf to stone, and a tail that can whip you like a truncheon, they can be pretty intimidating. They look to me like they should be stalking through the Jurassic underbrush tearing proto-mice limb from member.

In the 1980s when I was in vet school, iguanas suddenly became fashionable. No one, including veterinarians, knew much about them or seemed to understand why they became so popular. Ironically, at that time I was spending summers with my husband on the savannas of central Venezuela, where a team of researchers from the University of Tennessee happened to be carrying out some of the first field research on iguanas. I was at ground zero of late-breaking news on iguana biology. Maybe I could become an iguana specialist.

One of the surprises the researchers were finding was that despite their fierce demeanor, iguanas were more preyed upon than preying. The major preying is done by birds. For most of the year in Venezuela, you encounter iguanas lounging in piles on barren tree limbs arching out over ponds and lagoons. They may look asleep, but at slightest real or perceived threat, they bail out of the tree willy-nilly into the water. This is an excellent tactic for escaping aerial predators, but can be somewhat disconcerting for unsuspecting hikers, who, passing too close to an iguana tree, may be startled to find it suddenly raining iguanas.

A second line of defense is their breakaway tail. We've probably all seen the dime store lizard that cuts loose its two-inch tail if you grab it. It's quite another thing, though, to grab an iguana and find yourself holding two *feet* of writhing tail. To a predator it must be pretty disturbing to think that the lizard you grabbed had suddenly turned into a raging snake. The first time I did this by mistake in the clinic, I thought the tail would never stop twitching. Several times I believed it had stopped, but a quick touch started it going again, sending us stumbling back across the room to wait a little longer. Actually my technician was probably wondering whether the tail would stop twitching more than I was. I was wondering what I was going to say to the tail's human owner. "In South America iguana tail is something of a culinary delicacy…" No, that probably wasn't the right way to start off.

These defenses work pretty well for adult iguanas, but babies have it tough. During the dry season, females bury their eggs in the warm sand and by some synchronicity I don't pretend to understand, all the eggs from all the females hatch at about the same time. The savanna is suddenly swarming with four-inch iguana babies, which become *hors d'oeuvres* for the entire predator population. This evolutionary tactic, swamping predators for a brief period with more food than they can possibly eat, is common in species with young that are defenseless for only a short time. Wildebeests do the same thing in east Africa, dropping all their fawns at about the same time thus providing a moveable feast for hungry lions for a few days until the young wildebeests are capable of outrunning them.

In Venezuela, the savanna predators catch on to this newly hatched food in a hurry. Soon the caracaras (birds of prey, sort of a cross between a hawk and vulture) no longer lurk in the trees or soar on high, but amble across the savanna grazing on baby iguanas. Even our pet chicken Penny got into the act, racing across the yard to snatch them in her beak, smashing them on our concrete floor until sufficiently tenderized, then swallowing them whole. The only thing missing was a satisfied burp to finish off the meal.

One key finding of our friends studying the iguanas was that they ate only vegetation, mainly leaves. Of course, since they look so fierce and since most lizards with which people in the U.S. are familiar eat mainly insects, people generally assume that their pet iguana will thrive on a diet of flies, crickets, and mealworms. This is why I usually see them. Iguanas will eat just about anything—crickets, cornbread, coins, paper clips, rubber bands—so, as in humans, what they will eat is no guide at all to what they should eat. In fact, an insect diet leaves them so calcium-deficient that on X rays their bones are practically invisible, as if they've turned to rubber, which is pretty much what they've done. Owners bring me their iguanas because they don't seem to be moving right, or have stopped eating. I generally find they have multiple fractures of the legs or spine or "rubber jaw," which prevents them from chewing. At that time, before commercial iguana food was available, I'd recommend as diverse a diet of leafy green vegetables as possible and they seemed to do all right if their injuries were not already irreversible.

I also see iguanas fairly commonly for "problems of aggression," as we say. What this really means is that they attack their owner—which as I've pointed out can be pretty intimidating even to a hypercool, T-shirted, tattooed, and spiked-collar-wearing iguana owner. The reason also follows directly from iguana biology. During the breeding season, iguana males set up territories where females come to mate. No one, but no one, intrudes on their territory without suffering the consequences. Nadia could testify to that.

Nadia was not your typical iguana owner. That's the trouble with stereotypes. People are continually failing to live up to them. Nadia was an artsy type with a sixties look about her—tie-dye, sandals, and long straight hair. She was also wealthy enough to afford a large house on Nantucket Island and give over one entire room to Iggy, her pet iguana. She had fashioned for Iggy an enclosure on a jungle motif. Iggy's play area was an exquisite diorama consisting of artfully placed branches of authentic rainforest wood in the foreground merging into an imaginary jungle scene complete with parrots, palms, and agoutis in the background.

Iggy's problem was that he had suddenly begun attacking Nadia whenever she tried to enter his cage to feed him. This might have been problem enough with any iguana, but Iggy was huge, probably over five feet long, including the tail. Paint him dark gray and people might mistake him for a Komodo Dragon. He had severely lacerated Nadia's arm at least once, lashed her arms and legs black and blue with his tail, and even though she imagined that the fault was all hers, she realized that if she didn't do something Iggy was sure to land her in the hospital, or worse.

So she phoned for advice a well-known reptile veterinarian in California who happened to owe me one, because not long before I had referred Marshall, the fifty year old turtle, and Marshall's loony owner to him. I didn't know it, but she had been making his life a living hell ever since, hanging around the clinic at all hours, phoning him at home at night, blaming him for any and all new health problems that her geriatric turtle came down with. Your basic nightmare client.

However he didn't mention any of this. He simply said that he was referring an iguana owner in the Boston area to me. "I told her you were the best," he flattered me shamelessly over the phone, "She's got an aggressive male. I usually castrate them and that does the trick."

I should have been suspicious anyway. This was the same doctor who had decided that male iguanas attacked female owners only when they were menstruating. I'd heard similar stories about mountain lions and bears. The idea apparently is that males of any species will be incensed by women's reproductive secretions. That makes a lot of sense. I know that boars on the prowl and elephants in musth are pretty arousing to me. But he was the reptile expert, so I decided to not let this particularly strange hypothesis color my opinion of him too much.

At that time, I hadn't done much surgery on iguanas. I'd specialized in behavioral and dietary advice. In fact, I suspected that some of my behavioral advice might be warranted this time. One thing to do with an animal exhibiting territorial behavior is to disrupt his territory. Move his cage to a new room, for instance. Anything to make him feel less certain that the space where he happened to be really belonged to him.

Nadia wasn't having any of my behavioral advice. Move him? What about the diorama? The authentic rainforest wood? The jungle motif? That room unified the décor of the entire house. No, no, the great reptile expert in California who, did I forget, recommended me, had assured her that I would castrate Iggy and her problems would be solved.

Okay, how hard could it be? Iguanas, like birds, only have one developed testicle. Castrations are easy even with the standard two testicles. Fundamentally, you just make an incision, yank, tie, and snip.

Getting Iggy sedated was a challenge. Nadia had him in a crate that looked designed for a Saint Bernard and he just fit. It turned into your basic iguana rodeo, me with the heavy gloves being flung around the operating room while waiting for him to go under.

When I opened him up (iguanas have their testicle inside the body rather than in an external scrotum like most mammals) I imagined how my colleague, the renowned iguana expert, must have struggled to stifle his laughter as he advised me to castrate. Unlike a dog or cat, which has one major vein needing to be tied off per testicle, an iguana testicle turns out to be cradled in a basket of dozens of tiny veins, each of which needs to be tied off or he will bleed to death. Cursing and sweating, I watched the fifteen-minute surgery, which I'd booked into my schedule, turn into one hour, two hours, finally nearly three hours of nerve-wracking work. Iggy survived all right, but my waiting room was now spilling over with fuming clients, who were probably hoping that I wouldn't. I worked far into the night to finally catch up on my appointments, but my thoughts were occupied by thoughts of revenge.

For all the ordeal he went through, Iggy's behavior

wasn't improved by the operation. I tried to convince Nadia that since she wouldn't move him, perhaps she should trade Iggy for a new iguana, maybe a female. But she wouldn't hear of it, and I soon lost contact with her, although I kept my eye on the newspapers for an iguana owner done in by her pet.

I never was sure whether Nadia's reluctance to get rid of Iggy was due to obstinacy or love and devotion to her iguana. Asleep/awake and hungry/not hungry are about the only emotions I can detect in an iguana, and it's difficult to see how an owner could become too attached to them, although I know that people become attached to cars too.

I had no doubt that Sharon was devoted to her iguana, also named Iggy. I even grew fond of him myself. Fond enough to ruin a perfectly good Christmas for him in fact.

This Iggy, call him Iggy II, came to me with the typical dietary problems, stunted growth, and rubber jaw. He was in bad enough shape that I had to put him on a course of hormone therapy to increase his calcium absorption while at the same time adjusting his diet. His owner, Sharon, was a more typical iguana owner. With the grunge-iguana owner look, Sharon told me over the course of months of Iggy's treatment that she had had trouble meeting men until Iggy came into her life. Once he was healthy she had no trouble though. On weekends, she would lead Iggy II around Boston Common on a long leash and allow him to browse in the treetops. She got no end of attention doing this and soon had more men than she knew what to do with. The bond between Sharon and Iggy was truly touching. Tired of my injections, he would cling to Sharon like a newborn baby when she came to the office. When his treatment was over, he fairly leapt back into her arms and cuddled close.

Which made it all the more discouraging when Iggy II got dreadfully ill. He had the run of Sharon's house and had eaten something that blocked his digestive tract. I removed the obstruction surgically, but he was horribly infected by then. He went slowly down hill and died several days before Christmas.

On Christmas Eve, Sharon phoned to invite me to the funeral. The funeral? It was tomorrow, 10 A.M., at Heavenly Valley Memorial Pet Cemetery. Could I come?

Now I have nothing against people who have funerals for their pets. I'm not a big fan of funerals whether they are for people or pets. I'm the type that will pay some silent respects in my head and have done with it. But if funerals make people feel better about the passing of their loved ones, I'm all for them. I'd never been to a pet funeral before though, and had a little difficulty imagining what an iguana funeral on Christmas might be like.

My family was very understanding about me leaving for a few hours on Christmas Day. It wasn't all that unusual for me to have to go in to the hospital for a Christmas emergency anyway. Iggy II was laid out in a purple satin-lined casket shaped something like a pool cue case. The purple set off Iggy's green color nicely. A photograph of Iggy clambering about the trees of Boston Common leaned next to a candle on a small table nearby. The five of us,

Sharon, two friends of hers I didn't know, myself, and Iggy sat quietly for a while. Then each of the four humans said a few words, wept a few tears (me included). I think I said something about what a lucky animal Iggy was to have had such a wonderful owner. Then we followed as he was carried solemnly outside and lowered into the ground. It did manage to depress me which, like a lot of people, I don't need on Christmas.

Sharon got over her gloom quickly. She got a new iguana named Iggy, and fed him the right stuff from the get-go. He grew up green and sleek and healthy and was soon haunting the treetops of Boston Common like his predecessor. Sharon, so far as I know, never had trouble meeting men again.

Remember the iguana man hectoring my receptionist? He does fit into this picture. This happened to be on the day I castrated Iggy I. The waiting room crowd had gradually swelled while I labored in the operating room and the iguana man had finally snapped.

"Do you know how long I've been waiting?" He was shaking a box apparently containing his iguana in my receptionist's face. "Iggy needs immediate attention."

"What seems to be the problem here?" I put on my sternest doctorly tone. "Do you think you're the only one who has had to wait? Do you see anyone else acting like you? We can't plan for emergencies, you know." I was furious.

Then I looked in the box. This Iggy was lying on his side, eyes closed, feet stiffly in the air. I touched him. He was hard as a rock.

"When did you last notice Iggy move?" I asked sweetly.

"I don't know—a couple of days ago."

"Well, I don't know how to break this nicely but Iggy seems to be dead."

"Dead?"

"That's right, dead."

He took a moment to absorb the news, then went on the attack. "You killed him. I had to wait so long. I've been here since noon. He died right over there. I saw him roll over ten minutes ago. It's your fault. My lawyer will be in touch."

This was too much. I picked Iggy up by his tail. He was as stiff as a sword. Rigor takes longer to set in in reptiles than in mammals. He'd been dead for at least six hours, maybe a day. I waved Iggy in his face like a fly swatter. "Fine. And my lawyer will talk to your lawyer about animal neglect laws. Look at how thin he is. Did you ever feed him? Look. These legs look broken. So does his back. What did you beat him with?"

By this time, Iggy's owner was backing away, looking desperately around him for moral support. It wasn't forthcoming. Bless my clients. They were so wonderful in spite of the wait. He finally backed out the door, still issuing threats but you could tell his heart wasn't in it. This isn't something I'm necessarily proud of, but sometimes people have it coming.

CHAPTER 13

Ever See a Skeleton in a Tree?

A colleague of mine, a horse surgeon, came into the hospital one day looking a mess. His face looked like he had been dragged behind a bus, his arm was in a sling, and he was limping noticeably. "What happened," I asked, "forget to cinch your saddle?" He didn't answer. Sometimes my humor isn't appreciated. I later found out that he had fallen off a ladder while attempting to rescue a cat that appeared to be stranded high in one of the trees on his property. Good intention, dumb idea. Horse surgeons should stick to horses. I didn't tell him this.

Someone once asked me what sort of injuries cats got falling out of trees. "None," I said. In fact, I couldn't recall ever treating a cat for such injuries. If you want to know about injuries from cats stranded in trees, go to hospitals. It's the rescuers who get hurt, not the rescuees. If cats died when they climbed trees and were too frightened to get back down, where are the cat skeletons in trees?

Okay, cats do get hurt in falls, but not too often, not too badly, and not in falls from trees. Cat claws dig very firmly into wood, but not so firmly into steel or concrete.

Cats get hurt falling from high-rise buildings. There is even a technical term for such injuries—feline high-rise syndrome. New York City, not surprisingly, is the epicenter of feline highrise syndrome. When visiting, wear a sturdy hat.

A vet school friend of mine told me a horrible story that years after the fact made us both chuckle. As an undergraduate at Columbia, he had asked another student out on a date. She lived on the tenth or twelfth floor, I forget which, of an apartment building on 115th Street, right across from campus. When he arrived at her apartment, she wasn't quite ready, so he sat in the living room and waited. And waited. Her dog, a cute miniature schnauzer, came over and dropped a rubber ball at his feet. A dog lover, then as now, my friend couldn't resist and was soon tossing the ball across the room for the dog to retrieve. The dog was a fanatical and inexhaustible retriever. My friend tried bouncing the ball off the walls to see how well the dog handled rebound angles. Pretty well, indeed. He hadn't noticed it, but on a hot evening, his date, the dog's owner, had left the sliding door to the balcony part way open. One of his carom shots bounced through the opening, between the bars of the balcony's railing, and disappeared into the night sky. The schnauzer, closing in fast, disappeared right behind it.

There are some situations in life to which there is no good response. This was as close to such a situation as I can imagine. My friend did, as I probably would have, the only honorable thing—he tiptoed out the front door as quietly as he could and headed for the nearest bar. His most fervent wish in life, he decided after several drinks, was to never run into this particular woman again.

Dogs don't survive such incidents. Cats usually do. Cats fall more often too, thanks to their justified disdain for gravity. In what has become a rather famous study, veterinarians at New York City's Animal Medical Center years ago reported that of the 132 (!) cats that were admitted to their clinic for injuries from falls during a five month period, about 90 percent of them survived. These cats fell an average of a little more than six stories. The most fortunate (or unfortunate, depending on your point of view) cat plummeted thirty-two floors, nearly four hundred feet, and ended up with nothing much more than a chipped tooth. It didn't even break a leg, which is a common injury to high-rise cats.

Compare the success of cats with the failures of humans. It is almost unheard of for a human to survive a fall of even six stories onto a hard surface. Only about 1 percent of the more than twelve hundred people who have jumped off the Golden Gate Bridge (220 feet) survived, and they were landing in the water! This cat fell almost four hundred feet, landed on the pavement, and staggered away with minor injuries. What is it about cats?

At least three feline features conspire to make them so successful at surviving falls. First, their limbs are well-designed as shock absorbers, much better designed for that purpose than, say, dogs' or humans' limbs. After all, wild cats have lived in the trees for millions of years. Leaping up, jumping down, springing across, occasionally falling. That's life in the trees. A lifetime of such activities requires good shock absorbers and nature has provided them. You can see it if you watch how softly a cat seems to land even when jumping from a couch, compared to a dog or your rambunctious two-year-old.

Second, cats have that exquisite sense of equilibrium which is captured by the folk wisdom about them always landing on their feet. It's true. And landing on four good shock absorbers when falling spreads the shock nicely, leading to a much better outcome than landing on your side, back, front legs only, or head. There is even some evidence that in falls from heights greater than seven stories, after they've reached terminal velocity in other words, they spread their legs a bit, allowing their loose skin to act like a sort of parachute to slow their fall, something like a flying squirrel does. Cats falling from nine stories or more are less likely to fracture a leg than those falling seven stories or less.

One other thing I don't often mention concerns cats' brains. Brain trauma is the main cause of death from falls in humans, but cats are playing with a completely different (considerably smaller) deck. You often hear that cats are as smart as dogs, just more aloof. Don't believe it. As much as I love them, I have to admit that cats are brainstem animals. As long as the heart beats and the breathing continues, cat brains are doing about all the higher function they can. My old neurology professor, Dr. DelaHunta, loved to point out how a clogged midcerebral artery could leave almost half a cat's brain shriveled and shrunk like a rotting peach, yet the cat would be virtually unaffected. Usually the owners never noticed changes in behavior.

The final important factor is their small size. Despite Galileo's famous experiment in which falling cannon balls of different sizes all fell at the same rate, the rate at which objects less dense than cannon balls fall depends on their shape and their size. The resistance of air on the surface of a falling body determines its terminal velocity—the maximum speed it will reach. Cats max out at about sixty miles per hour whether they fall six or six hundred stories. Humans, being larger, therefore having less surface area for their weight, double that. And 120 miles per hour for a falling human is terminal indeed.

Size also counts at the bottom, the business end of a fall—"It's not the fall that kills you, it's the sudden stop." There's more than a little truth to this hackneyed witticism. Momentum is what does the damage when a moving body encounters an immovable surface. Momentum is mass times velocity. Cats, falling slower than humans, also hit with less momentum due to their lighter weight. Biologist J.B.S. Haldane sums up this dry physics rather nicely, "You can drop a mouse down a thousand-yard mine shaft; and, on arriving at the bottom, it gets a slight shock and walks away. A rat is killed, a man is broken, a horse splashes."

Which brings us to back to cats in trees. Why do they ever get stuck in trees when they could likely fall many times farther and be unharmed? Well, usually it's a kitten thing. Young cats lack experience and presence of mind. They lose focus, climb higher than they realize, look down, and start to worry in a very vocal fashion. But if a misguided human attempts to lift them off their nice secure branch, that worry turns to desperation and panic, much to the hazard of the would-be rescuer. If you want to see a normally placid cat turn before your eyes into a wild-eyed, spitting, hissing whirlwind of slashing claws and canines, try to lift it off a high tree limb against its will. If left alone, of course, eventually the cat works out its anxiety and makes its way back down.

So what about tigers in trees? This seemingly absurd question became suddenly very relevant to Steve one sunny day when he worked as a large cat trainer for the movies.

"Steve!" He heard alarm in the voice of Tippi, his boss's wife. "Ivan is stuck in a tree. Will you get him down?"

Ivan was a young Siberian tiger.

At about six months of age, Ivan was a nice enough tiger under normal circumstances, probably weighing no more than one hundred or 120 pounds. But that was a little large for lifting off a tree limb by the scruff of his neck while perched on top of a wobbly ladder. Worse, Ivan was Tippi's favorite. Steve had had a secret crush on Tippi ever since he had first seen her star in the movie *The Birds* when he was a teenager. Now that he knew her personally, he found that he also respected her deeply as a warm and kind and caring human being. He felt obligated to make some heroic effort on her behalf. With a leaden sense of dread he went to check out the situation.

There was Ivan, all right—flat on his belly on a stout lower branch of a large cottonwood, no more than twenty or thirty feet off the ground. The branch drooped over the edge of a shallow pond. Ivan was braying loudly, the tiger equivalent of a worried cat's meow.

Steve considered the possibilities. He had a ladder tall enough to lean against the branch itself. He could place it near Ivan, climb up from almost directly under him, and...then what? On the other hand, he could lean the ladder against the tree trunk, climb up to the branch, and inch his way out along it, so that Ivan would have plenty of opportunity to escalate his current worry to white-eyed panic. Steve had once tried this approach with a neighborhood kitten and got pretty scratched up for his efforts. That kitten weighed a pound, maybe a pound and a half. There sprawled Ivan, roughly a hundred times bigger. Steve screwed up his courage and made his decision.

"Tippi, Ivan got up there by himself, he can get down by himself. We just have to wait until his hunger overcomes his fear. He'll be down by dark, I promise you."

Tippi looked crestfallen. He could tell that his personal stock with her had plummeted. He felt like a terrible failure—a living, healthy failure though. Sweet person that she is, she didn't plead or threaten or insist. Instead, she went looking for the other trainer, whom out of pity I'll call Brad.

Brad, who had had more years of animal training experience than Steve and who therefore might have been expected to make better decisions, also had a bit of a crush on Tippi. In fact, he must have thought more highly of her than Steve did, because the next thing you knew he was inching out along Ivan's branch, reassuring him that he had nothing to fear and that help was on its way.

This wasn't the way Ivan saw it. His eyes grew wide even as Brad climbed the ladder. Now he spun to face him, and began seriously snarling and snapping, gripping the tree even more tightly with his claws while beginning to inch backwards toward the end of the branch. Brad inched closer, Ivan inched back. Brad reassured him some more and inched closer still. The branch began to bend and sway. Ivan had backed up as far as he could. He looked over his shoulder. Snarling ever more loudly, he glared at Brad and suddenly made a short, very quick swipe. "Aaaaaaaaaaaaaaah," Brad tumbled out of the tree, landing with a splash in the pond. He was on his feet immediately, both hands covering his face, blood seeping out between his fingers. "My eye! I can't see! He got my eye!"

Steve, who had been watching the whole proceedings with mounting disbelief, had already thought about warming up the pickup truck to make the inevitable dash to the hospital (an hour away) as fast as possible. But he kept hoping that Brad would come to his senses as he saw Ivan gradually losing grip on his sanity. Now Steve rushed over to see if he could be of any belated help.

It took quite a while before Brad quieted down and would take his hands away from his face. He seemed to have the irrational hope that maybe his eye would be all right if he just held it in place long enough. When he was finally coaxed to let Steve have a look, the news was remarkably good. One of Ivan's claws had sliced him just below the eye. The laceration was neither very long nor very deep—just deep enough to cause blood to well up into his eye making him think that the eye itself was gone. A few stitches, antibiotics, and he would be fine.

The trip to the hospital was not particularly enjoyable for Brad, who, in addition to the pain from the cut and the bumps and bruised from his fall from the tree, had to listen to Steve's exhaustive and repeated analyses about how stupid it had been to try to get a tiger out of a tree.

When they returned late in the afternoon, the tree was empty. Ivan was playing with his sister Natasha at the water's edge. After a call from the hospital had assured her that Brad would be all right, Tippi had gone home, leaving a note thanking him for his efforts.

Ivan *foofed* a greeting to Brad as he entered the compound and rubbed up against him affectionately to show that there were no hard feelings. Then he began cavorting in circles—inviting Brad to play. Brad didn't feel like playing.

Steve and Brad began to load up the wheelbarrows with chicken necks for the evening feeding. This was usually the nicest part of the day. The air had cooled, the mountains were bathed in pink by the setting sun, the echoes of the roars of fifty hungry lions resounded down the canyon. "I bet you never heard of feline high-rise syndrome." Steve began to push the wheelbarrow. "Cats fall out of buildings, not out of trees..." Brad's bad day was not over yet.

CHAPTER 14

At Least I'm Not Hung Up about It

"*Mister* Moore, what am I holding in my hand?"

"Those would be testicles, Dr. King."

"A good start, Mr. Moore. And what do they come from?"

John King was one of my favorite professors in vet school. A rough-hewn, handsome man reminding me of Anthony Quinn in the movie *Zorba the Greek*, his Friday afternoon grand rounds were legendary. The bleachers surrounding his own personal theater-in-the-round, a gleaming tile-floored morgue in Cornell's pathology department, were invariably filled to overflowing. He was more entertaining than the circus, plus you never left without having learned a lot. Arriving late was to be avoided at all costs though. The only remaining seats would be in the front. Students, even other professors, would pack into the standing room behind the bleachers rather than sit up front. Those were the inquisition seats. Dr. King taught the old-fashioned way, putting students on the spot in front of their peers. I was one of his favorite victims.

John is a pathologist. It was his job to teach us the detective work of medicine, how to interpret autopsy, or as they are called in animals, necropsy findings. "The dead talk to the living," I remember him saying. "You need to learn the language of the dead to hear what they have to say. No matter how good or how careful you are, you will make mistakes during your career. You will kill animals because of those mistakes. Good pathology will help you learn from those mistakes. That's what is important."

John loved teaching, did it superbly, and became more than a professor to many of us. He became a friend. His other passion in life, besides teaching pathology, was rock-climbing. Thursday afternoons he would head out to some of the better climbing spots near campus with a group of students who wanted to relieve some of the pressures of school with a little physical excitement. I'd done quite a bit of climbing in my undergraduate years, and for some reason never had had any fear of heights. This was probably why he and I hit it off right away. He might think he could intimidate me in the classroom, but he very clearly couldn't on shale precipices around Ithaca.

Striding through the door exactly as the four o'clock bell sounded, carrying large white buckets filled with the most interesting animal organs of the week, he had the dramatic flair and timing of an actor.

"We're all waiting, Mr. Moore. What do they come from?" He paced back and forth along the bleachers holding the organs aloft like an attorney addressing a jury.

My poor classmate wasn't sure. Neither was I. They were huge. A bull, maybe? A horse? I'd come in a little late, but wasn't about to push my way to the front until this testicle issue was resolved.

"A...a horse?" Moore stammered.

"Ah, a horse. Mr. Moore thinks these balls belong to a horse," John shook his head in disappointment. "Does anyone else have a better idea? Miss Tolchin, you specialize in large animals. What do you think? Do these look like horses' balls to you?"

Pat Tolchin, one of my brightest classmates, was not going to be intimidated. She could dish it out and take it. She was one of John's favorite victims too.

"No sir, I believe they are from a sheep. My guess would be a male, a pretty small one at that." That got a laugh from the gallery.

"A male, eh? Excellent insight. I see your knowledge of anatomy is stunning," John chuckled. "You're right about the species too. It is from a ram. Small, though? I don't know about small. That ram, I can tell you, weighed 180 pounds." He paused. "*I* weigh about 180 pounds." He hefted the testicles a little higher in his hand and thought a moment. "I don't think it's fair." That got an even bigger laugh.

Pathologists, not surprisingly, have unusual senses of humor. I probably would too if I spent all my time dissecting the dead. I remember a few years ago a county coroner somewhere in the U.S. got in trouble because his aides reported some of his more gruesome jokes about airplane crashes and celebrity autopsies. But humor can be a way of easing tension. A lot of surgeons make jokes that might otherwise be considered tasteless too while they are operating. You do what you need to do.

In my freshman year, John once tried to fluster me as he had tried to do with Pat. He particularly liked to put new freshmen on the spot. That told him right away which ones were going to be the best fodder for his repartee in later years, which ones he could use to best purpose for entertaining and enlightening the others, and also which ones would clam up in embarrassment forever after. He had to find another approach with those students.

I had arrived a bit late that time as well. I was working in the bird clinic already and had to check on a patient before heading over to the pathology department. I didn't yet know about avoiding the front bleacher row, and so caused a bit of stir in the crowd as I settled in directly in front of him as he was presenting his first case. A similar stir might be made in a crowd watching someone unknowingly step in front of a speeding bus.

"Ah, who have we here? Your name, dear?" He was all mock innocence. I wasn't even sure if he was talking to me, a lowly freshman.

"Me? I'm a new freshman, Veronika Kiklevich. Sorry I'm late, I was…"

"It's all right, Miss Kiklevich. We don't mind if you're late. We're all busy here too. We only mind if you can't tell me what I'm holding?" His hand was inches from my nose.

I looked around for help. None was forthcoming. I was a freshman for heaven's sake, how was I supposed to know this stuff? My eyes began to water from the smell of the formalin dripping off his gloves. I hoped it didn't look like I was weeping. I finally focused on what he was holding. "Those are balls, Dr. King."

"Yes, well actually here we call them testicles, Miss Kiklevich, but that's very good. In fact before you arrived, Mr. Goodwin had just finished identifying these as testicles from a moderately large dog. A German shepherd, actually. Now can you tell me why I am holding them when they should be bouncing about at home in their own little scrotum?"

"Castration? The dog came in to be neutered?" How was I supposed to know?

"*Miss* Kiklevich, would I have something as commonplace as healthy testicles, removed in a routine castration, for the week's pathology grand rounds? I try to introduce students to unusual and intriguing pathology. To teach them something they won't learn from books. What would they—what would you—learn by looking at healthy testicles? Now *look* at this one and tell me what you see."

The silence began to seem a bit deafening. I got the feeling that how I reacted here might have a lot to do with how well I got by in vet school for the next four years. I decided that I might be right or I might be wrong, but I was not going to be intimidated. I snatched the testicle from him and inspected it carefully from all sides. It looked normal enough to me except there were two small punctures running completely through it, like it had been stabbed by hypodermic syringes. I handed it back.

"Well, Miss Kiklevich, what have you to say?"

"There are two puncture wounds, otherwise it looks normal, so I would guess…" I thought desperately, "…snakebite."

117

It brought the house down. Even John couldn't stifle a chuckle. "All right, Miss Kiklevich, that's a reasonable hypothesis. Reasonable, but wrong. Not snakebite, but shotgun would be the correct answer. A good attempt though. From now on, I'd advise you not to handle formalinized material without gloves. Please wash your hands in that sink and we'll hope to see you sitting in the same spot next week."

From that point on, we became good friends. During my senior year, John had a climbing accident thanks to an error by a novice student climber. Thank goodness it wasn't fatal. He broke both heels rather badly, and there were no pathology grand rounds for many months, a major disappointment to me. John is retired now. I'm sure his wonderfully colorful and memorable teaching style would not be appreciated, probably not even tolerated, today. It's a shame.

I don't know why it is, but when I think now of all the interesting cases John presented in those pathology rounds, parading around with lungs or livers or brains held dramatically aloft, explaining to us what had gone wrong with them, the only ones I seem to remember are the testicle cases. It must be because guys, my male professors and classmates, always made such a to-do about male genitalia, as do my many of my male clients today. I only have to mention that maybe castration would perhaps be the best medical decision for their animal to watch men begin to squirm and hem and haw.

What is it that makes men personalize these things so? Women don't react similarly when I mention "spay." I wish I had a dollar for all the animals that didn't get neutered because their male owners had a weird attitude about castration. Even the fact that we use the euphemism "neuter" rather than "castrate" says a lot about male sensitivity on the subject. It's true that we call it a "spay" rather than an "ovariohysterectomy" in females, but that's more to avoid the polysyllabic mouthful rather than avoid picturing about the procedure itself. "Neuter" on the other hand has exactly the same number of syllables as "castrate," but is just a much vaguer term. You figure it out.

Sometimes these sensitivities have real-life consequences. So for instance, Mary owned a wonderful standard poodle named LaBete, which had developed prostate problems as he had gotten older. First, he had a series of prostatic infections which I managed to treat with antibiotics, but his prostate also gradually enlarged. Eventually it enlarged dramatically, from the normal walnut size to about the size of a grapefruit.

Intact dogs, like humans, often develop enlarged prostates as they age. However most elderly dogs have been castrated. Castration cuts off the hormonal support needed to maintain the prostate, so it shrinks away to nothing. This is one reason that treatment of prostate ailments is not a major medical condition in geriatric dogs. If we do see an elderly dog with prostate problems, it is either because the animal was once a valuable breeder or because the owner has a hang-up about castration and never had the dog fixed when it was young.

This latter was the case with LaBete. You might have known from its name. It apparently means "The Beast" in

French—an odd name for such a lovable animal as a standard poodle. Mary's husband Dale, a hotshot liability attorney as I recall, had come up with the name. He must have hoped LaBete would turn out to be an intimidating guard dog instead of the sweetie that he was. However, Dale, even after LaBete began developing these problems, could never bring himself to allow his boy to be castrated as I suggested.

Dogs' plumbing is a bit different than humans. An enlarged prostate in a human tends to constrict the urethra, making urinating difficult. In a dog it gradually blocks the bowel, making it difficult—eventually impossible—to have a bowel movement. This was the stage that LaBete was at. At times he had become so constipated that he groaned in pain for hours at a time, until with enemas and laxatives, we could give him some relief. His abdomen had the firmness of a watermelon. I was also worried that the enlarged prostate might ultimately turn cancerous. "It's going to eventually kill him if we don't do something," I told Mary. I also let her know that prostate surgery is a major invasive procedure, full of danger for an older dog. If I castrated him, even at his age, LaBete's prostate would shrink away to nothing within a matter of weeks.

"No," she assured me, "Dale would never stand for it." I offered to talk with Dale about it. "No," she now looked even more worried, "that wouldn't be advisable."

I had an idea. "Have you ever heard of Neuticles?" Neuticles are artificial replacement testicles for dogs whose owners felt that castration would destroy their animals' self-confidence and self-esteem. Their developer, Gregg Miller, had apparently been surprised to learn that when a male was neutered it meant that its testicles were permanently removed. He discovered this when his beloved bloodhound Buck was neutered. He worried that Buck "would no longer be Buck," so he set about developing Neuticles. His company, CTI (Canine Testicular Implant) Corporation, now manufactures Neuticles for cats, dogs, bulls, horses, and, soon, monkeys. They also sell Neuticle keychains, T-shirts, and baseball caps. The implants come in three models, Neuticles Original (polypropylene, hard as a marble), Neuticles Natural (silicon, with "actual pet testicle firmness"), and Neuticles Ultra (silicon but 30 percent softer than the real thing, for who knows what reason). According to company literature, the first Neuticle implant in 1995 was hailed by *Parade* magazine as one of the top ten news events of the year. I don't remember a lot of news events from 1995, but it must have been a pretty slow year for news.

Canine Neuticles come in five sizes, petite, extra small, small, medium, and large. These names reveal that marketing sophistication has not yet reached Buckner Missouri, corporate headquarters of CTI. In the future, given their clientele, I'm sure these sizes will be renamed regular, large, extra large, super extra large, and humongous. A group of my female veterinarian friends and I had been making backroom jokes about Neuticles for years. One of them had even regaled us about having to disqualify an entry at a large dog show when she found the dog had three testicles—two regular ones plus a Neuticle.

In some endeavors, mathematical literacy is critical. Now, it seemed, I had my first potential Neuticle user.

Mary was immediately interested. Would they look just like the real thing? Might a close observer notice anything different? No, I assured her, after a few weeks when the surgical signs disappear you'd never know the difference. Now that Neuticles Natural were available, they even *felt* the same if someone were inclined to check it out in detail.

"All right! Let's do it," she enthused. "Dale and I are going to Europe next week. I'll drop LaBete off to board while we're gone and when we get back he'll never know."

"Who'll never know?" I suddenly didn't have such a good feeling about my idea.

"Dale," she said. "He'd never agree, but what he doesn't know won't hurt him."

I was sorely tempted. Dale probably would never know. The dog would be healthy again and out of pain by the time they returned. But there were some problems. The first was an ethical issue. Even though getting permission from Mary would probably absolve me of legal liability, was it right to perform a medical procedure on a pet when all its owners had not agreed to it? More than that, when I had very good reason to suspect that one of the owners would actively object to it. On a more practical level, I didn't know Dale, had never even spoken with him on the phone. Mary seemed a bit afraid of him and he obviously had some deep issues with having his dog castrated. Did I need to chance that some maniac might end up stalking me because I castrated his dog behind his back?

Despite Mary's misgivings, I told her I needed to speak with Dale before going ahead with the surgery. I phoned him that night at home and launched into a long explanation of the advantages of castration for dogs in general, and for LaBete specifically. I emphasized that the only reasonable way to cure LaBete's problem was not to try some drastic surgery that the dog possibly wouldn't survive, but a simple procedure that took a few minutes, was perfectly safe with rapid recovery, and thanks to the development of a new product, no one would ever know he had undergone.

Up to the last part, he hadn't said a word. I wasn't sure whether he was still listening or had put the phone down and had walked away. But in fact he was there all along, because he now started firing questions at me. What sort of product did I mean? What were they made out of? Would there be telltale scars? Did they look real? Or obviously fake like prosthetic eye implants?

Now that I was sure that I had his attention, I spent a few more minutes describing Neuticles and their implantation in detail—the various sizes, textures, the realistic weight, the lack of surgical complications. I felt he was almost ready to agree.

"I've got just one more question, Doc," he finally said. "You say they come in different sizes depending on the size of your dog?"

Yes, I assured him, that's correct. LaBete, at about fifty pounds, would be a canine regular.

"Okay, okay. Sounds like the right thing to do. Go ahead. I'll tell Mary I don't mind. There's one other thing, though. Any chance we could move up a size for LaBete?"

Wouldn't you know?

I told him no. There's only so much room inside the scrotum. We wanted LaBete to be comfortable, didn't we? He would have to be a regular. The surgery went off without a hitch and LaBete has lived a comfortable healthy life to this day.

By now I've told this story a lot to my female friends when I felt like making fun of some men's obsessions with that one precious body part of theirs. I have to admit, I do make fun of such things pretty often. However I know of at least one man who must assume that it's not really the men, but it's me who has an obsession with male genitalia. I certainly wouldn't want my female friends talking to him. This man is Dr. Chuck Leathers, chief pathologist where I now work. I'm not sure that I've ever looked him straight in the eye in recent years. I've tried, but I can't.

Not long after Steve and I first moved west to the rolling hills along the Idaho-Washington border, I made my *faux pas*. I had settled in quickly at my new job as a clinical instructor at the veterinary college. I found that I enjoyed the teaching part of my job almost as much as the clinical work. Plus, with all the specialists at a such a large teaching hospital, I was learning a tremendous amount myself.

One day, Dr. Leathers phoned me with a pathology report. I hadn't formally met him yet. We'd passed in the corridors occasionally, but except for perfunctory greetings we'd never had a real conversation. Chuck generally has a noncommittal, even stern, expression. He's not prone to the social smile, which might put someone new immediately at ease. In my experience such people are usually either really dour and humorless, or else possess an acutely deadpan sense of humor. I didn't know it at the time, but Chuck really is a deadpan humorist. One of the funniest people I know, in fact. He is a pathologist, though, so his sense of humor is not that of your average person.

But at the time I didn't know this, and from all reports that I had heard about him, I only knew that he was immensely knowledgable. Noncommital, nonsmiling, and knowledgable. Just the sort of person, in other words, who tends to foster my insecurities.

After explaining the case he had phoned about, he casually asked, "By the way, will your husband be sending me any more opossum penises?"

Even from a pathologist, this question came as a surprise. I knew that Steve had been having some trouble in the opossum colony he used in his aging research. There had been an outbreak of flesh-eating bacteria in the colony. Several animals had died and I knew that Dr. Leathers had done necropsies on them. But penises? Why not pancreases? Maybe this was some odd way of breaking the ice with new doctors.

When I'm nervous I sometimes have an unfortunate tendency to babble—particularly if the person on the other end of the conversation remains silent. I was nervous now. Opossum penises, eh?

"Yes, he probably will. Aren't they odd? You probably noticed they're forked. That's why people used to think that males copulated with the female's nose. That blue scrotum, it's pretty bizarre too. Bat penises are even odder. I used to take care of a bat colony and the males would threaten you with an erection that came clear up to their chin. Have you seen the interns' room? They've got a huge wall poster with penises of the animal world. Hippos, chimps, kangaroos. Some of the strangest shapes you've ever seen. Not as strange as the chicken flea penis though. That's a mechanical masterpiece."

Even as I continued talking to Dr. Leathers, I was thinking, "Stop. Enough already." But I was too nervous to help myself. I had recently happened to flip through a book of Steve's on the evolution of animal genitalia. This was how I knew about the chicken flea. But I wasn't finished yet.

"Of course, entomologists use penis shape to help classify different species. Did you ever wonder why we don't do this in mammals? You could if you wanted. In fact, I think bat people do use penis size and shape for the same thing. I'm sure of it now. Yes, one of my college professors had a collection of bat bacula—penis bones—now that I think about it. Couldn't do it in spiders though. They don't have penises. Just those pedipalps which they use for the same thing. Copulation, I mean. They come in the oddest sizes and shapes too, especially when they're expanded. Steve did his Ph.D. on spiders. That's how I know. Oh well, thanks for calling. I'll tell Steve that you asked."

As I set down the phone rather breathlessly, it seemed as if Dr. Leather's "good-bye" had sounded at bit puzzled. Then I suddenly realized that he hadn't asked about penises at all. He had asked whether my husband was going to send him any more opossum *pieces*. Pieces, not penises. Oh my God, what had I done?

From now on, of course, I had to plan my day around avoiding Dr. Leathers. I asked interns to take his calls for me, detoured around corridors where I worried we might have a chance encounter, even began parking in a distant parking lot. Naturally, the story got out. I probably mentioned it to a student in explaining why I was taking such a circuitous route to my office. That student must have told other students. All of the students, if not all of the hospital, soon knew. So that wasn't the end of it.

Not long after, I was caring for an ostrich after some complicated orthopedic surgery. Ostriches aren't common in the hospital, so a gaggle of students accompanied me every time I treated it. Unfortunately, it developed post-surgical problems and died a few days later. I asked a student to fill out the paperwork to send to pathology. We had to know why it had died in case we ever did more surgery on ostriches. After avoiding phone calls about the ostrich from Dr. Leathers in the days following, I finally got the pathology report in the mail. In reading it, I noticed that someone, no doubt a student, had added a sentence to the original orders, "Please examine the penis carefully," and signed my name.

CHAPTER 15

A Pack of Trouble

A puppy is not a dog. But a puppy becomes a dog. A dog is not a wolf. But dogs once were wolves. These statements may seem obvious, but they pretty much summarize what it's taken me nearly twenty years of veterinary practice to learn about applied animal behavior. Some people have to learn these lessons the hard way. I was lucky. I learned them the easy way. It's helped make me a better doctor.

As a naïve young veterinarian, I was proud of my medical knowledge, my facility at explaining complex medical problems to laypeople, my more than passable surgical skills. Complacency is an impediment to learning. So it took me a lot longer than it should have to learn that rather than focusing all my attention on the animal, I could frequently get more insight into animals just by watching the way they interacted with their owner, their owner's children if they came along, or with me in the treatment room.

For instance, do the clients think it is cute to allow the St. Bernard puppy to stand up on them or rush across the room to leap into their lap? If so, I'm looking at future problems—an unhappy, potentially dangerous pet, unhappy, potentially injured owners, frustration and confusion all around. It doesn't have to be this way.

The obvious problem in that scenario is that a ten-pound St. Bernard puppy will before long be a 180-pound adult whose owner has taught it that he enjoys being assaulted in this way. Steve, in his lion training days, had a lot of experience with the phenomenon in which people somehow can't picture a cute youngster as a large adult. One of the most common questions he got at Hollywood parties was, "My eight-year-old daughter loves lions. Do you know where I can buy a lion cub?" Even though he would discourage them as strongly as he could, and give them no information about where to buy one, they would sometimes manage to locate one anyway. Then, six months later, would come the panicked call about the lion not allowing them into their own bedroom, or killing their dog, or attacking their daughter or the neighbor. Unfortunately, it is usually innocent bystanders who get hurt for some rather obvious reasons that I'll get to shortly.

There was even one man I'll call Gordon, who should have known better because he used to hang out with the trainers at the lion compound where Steve worked. He had watched professional trainers just enough to imagine that he too knew how to train big cats and the next thing you knew he had purchased a tiger cub. Without telling anyone, he was training it at home to jump into his arms on command.

One day he brought Samba with him to visit the compound and showed everyone his new trick.

Crouching and clapping his hands, he would shout, "Jump, Samba," and little Samba would spring into his waiting arms. Very cute, indeed. A few months later, of course, came the panicked call. Gordon was trapped in his bathroom, afraid to come out. Steve agreed to take Samba off his hands for a few weeks to attempt a little remedial training. He was worried that it might be too late though.

It turned out that it was too late. At his first training session, Samba made a lunge for a visiting photographer who was shooting pictures of some of the other animals. Fortunately, Steve had Samba on a chain leash and managed to jerk him off balance just enough to make him miss the photographer. Jack Rabin's wife Dorothy wasn't so lucky. Jack was one of the workers hired to clean cages. His qualification for the job was that he had two pet lions and they hadn't killed anyone yet. This deluded him into thinking he was highly knowledgable about big cats in general. Dealing exclusively with his own animals had made him overconfident and sloppy in his precautions, though. Cleaning Samba's cage one day, he asked his wife to step inside to keep him company. She foolishly did so, and the next thing you knew Samba had her on the ground with her head and neck in his mouth. He may have been careless, but you couldn't accuse Jack of lacking guts. He leapt on to Samba's back, pried his jaws apart with his bare hands, and ordered his prostrate wife to get out. She managed to crawl to safety, but the damage had been done. Plastic surgery removed most of her facial scars, but nothing could be done about the damage to her seventh cranial nerve, which left her with a sagging, paralyzed face on one side. The psychic damage was probably just as severe. She and Jack divorced soon after.

The problem in these scenarios is not simply one of size—the little animal grows into a bigger animal, making previously cute behavior dangerous. The problem is dominance too. As an animal grows, it has a natural tendency to find out where it fits in the local dominance hierarchy. The only way to find this out is by testing the hierarchy. I learned a lot about hierarchy testing from the Winchester wolf pack.

There's some inescapable aura associated with wolves. People seem to either fear or love them, or fear *and* love them. No one seems disinterested. Nevertheless, a casual acquaintance with real wolves makes it pretty obvious they would not make safe pets, so wolf-dog hybrids have become relatively popular pets instead. As I said, no one is disinterested in wolves, so there have arisen formal wolf-hybrid associations to promote them as pets, and there have also arisen anti-wolf-hybrid associations to promote the opinion that a wolf-dog hybrid is a dangerous abomination. I've had a lot of experience with wolf-dog hybrids. Albuquerque seemed to be full of them. If properly trained, they make decent pets—"if properly trained" being the operative phrase. Most of the time, it isn't an issue, because the majority of wolf hybrids I see are not that at all. They are husky-malamute crosses or shepherd-husky crosses, which have been sold as wolf hybrids. The owners rarely believe me when I tell them that their animal has none of the anatomical features that define a real wolf hybrid. If they paid lots of money for it, it has to be the real thing. Ironically, these fake hybrids are usually more aggressive, and less manageable, than the real ones. This is clearly due to training, or more specifically, *lack* of training. I think owners of fake hybrids probably subconsciously imagine that a poorly trained, aggressive dog is more authentically wolf-like.

But neither dogs nor wolf hybrids are the real thing. The real thing has longer legs, a bit of a pigeon-toed stance, more forward-directed eyes, and massive teeth compared to a dog or even a hybrid of similar size. As a specialist in veterinary dentistry, I'm mightily impressed every time I look at the huge teeth and tooth roots wolves possess. The real thing also has a considerably more prickly disposition.

I became the veterinarian for the Winchester wolf pack by chance. The pack manager at the time, Meegan, phoned the veterinary college looking for a doctor who did exotic animal medicine. I was the logical candidate. I wasn't sure that I was interested though. It sounded intriguing, but I was already beginning to be overwhelmed with work at my new job. I was not seeing Steve and the kids as much as I would like to either. Did I need another unpaid professional duty?

But the first time I drove down to Winchester, Idaho, (population 308) to see the wolves, I knew I would agree to be their doctor. It was a brisk and bright fall afternoon. The drive itself was divinely scenic, down the Clearwater Breaks, along Lapwai Creek, into the mountains on the Nez Perce Reservation. The wolves had a lovely place to live—twenty-two acres of scattered pines, firs, and underbrush, a small creek, all surrounded by a shiny, new double chainlink fence. The inside fence was twelve feet high with an electric wire running around the top, the outer fence was ten feet high. These people took security seriously. I liked that. Meegan lived just outside the compound in a cozy *ger*, the traditional circular felt tent of Mongolia. I felt like I had stepped into another world.

The pack, seven males and four females, had been assembled from several captive sources for the making of nature documentaries. Once filming had ended, the producer decided to keep the pack together for scientific research and education. There were a handful of such captive wolf packs scattered around the country. Scientists could systematically study the behavior of the wolves, and the public could visit them to learn more about these elusive carnivores. Perhaps they would become interested in wolf conservation issues, which is a hot topic in the rural northwest.

Originally located at a remote site in the Sawtooth Mountains, the Nez Perce Indians eventually agreed to accept the pack permanently on their reservation. Contact with animals native to their traditional homeland was important to them. When the wolves first moved to Winchester, the Nez Perce had a welcoming ceremony and planned in subsequent years to gradually integrate the wolves into some of their traditional rituals. The Wolf Education and Research Center, as it came to be called, had a governing board composed of volunteers with a passion for, and extensive knowledge of, wolves. The board made all major decisions concerning the general management of the pack. Meegan made day-to-day decisions.

My first experience with the pack consisted of nothing more than watching them from outside the fence, seeing what I could discern about their health from a distance. The first thing that struck me is that a wolf pack is a very tense society, kind of like a group of overstressed executives might be if they were strung out on amphetamines and locked together in a small meeting room, forced to reach a consensus decision. Social status, who is dominant to whom, is the essence of pack life. Despite various elaborate appeasement displays and relatively nonviolent means to assert dominance, there was always enough sniping and jostling for status, that small wounds, miscellaneous rips and tears, were ubiquitous even in the most settled of times. If there were any social upheaval in the pack, wound number and severity shot up. There was even a characteristic wound I called the "omega patch." The omega animal is the lowest ranked animal as the alpha is the highest ranked. The omega can be bitten by everyone, and dares bite no one in return. Consequently, the omega always has bloody rump wounds—the omega patch. One omega female eventually died when one of the wounds got badly infected. The board's opinion was that we shouldn't intervene medically except under exceptional conditions.

Having seen the pack in action, my first real medical experience with them had to do with sterilizing the females. One female had already delivered a litter, which had led to a board decision to make the pack nonreproductive in the future. Because hormones affect behavior, and doing a normal spay removes the ovaries and thus ovarian hormones, it was decided we should sterilize them by tying off the oviducts, in other words, tying their tubes. They would be sterile, but their hormones would be unaffected.

In a group of dogs this would be easy. Remove one from the group, do the surgery, wait for her to recover, put her back with the group. But in a wolf pack, the status quo is constantly being challenged. Any sign of weakness will be immediately exploited by subordinates. A chance injury, illness, or old age may lead to the sudden defeat and even death. Simply removing an animal from the pack for a time might cause all sorts of social disruption. Returning a groggy, post-surgical female to the pack might ensure her death. Our key medical challenge, then, was to anesthetize and operate on all the females without upsetting the pack dynamics among the males or females. We didn't want to allow, for instance, a low-ranking female to try to usurp the alpha female's place because she had been temporarily removed. Nor did we want a woozy wolf to have her dominance status permanently altered by an aggressive male or a female who had happened to recover from surgery more quickly.

This job was clearly beyond the capabilities of a lone doctor. I decided that my best approach was to assemble a team—become the medical impresario. Fortunately, I had a host of friends to impose upon at the vet school. Over the next couple of weeks, I enlisted two outstanding surgeons, one anesthesiologist, four technicians, and myself to do the job. We all showed up on a frosty fall morning. The previous afternoon, Meegan's staff had separated the four females from the rest of the pack, isolating them inside a separate one-acre enclosure adjacent to the main compound.

The procedures went off like clockwork. We anaesthetized them all at about the same instant, four injections synchronized like a firing squad. Then each sleeping female was placed on a large piece of plywood, which when propped across the handlebars and seat of the all-terrain vehicles (which the staff used for bush transportation) became our operating tables. There were two ATVs, so we could do two surgeries at a time. Dr. Tobias, a surgical genius, did the job, from first incision to last suture, in seventeen minutes flat. Dr. Cambridge came in a hair behind her. Less than an hour after their original injections, all four females were beginning to awaken from the anesthesia. Each animal was watched over and reassured during the recovery period by one of Meegan's staff whom the wolves knew. By early afternoon, they were fully alert. We released them back into the main compound. Meegan reported to me the amount of social disruption the procedure had caused over the next few days. That was easy. She just had to do a wound count. The disruption, I was pleased to learn, had been minimal.

But human disruptions aren't the only ones. Natural disruptions occur as well. A couple of years later, things had changed. Meegan had moved on. The new pack manager was Jeremy. One day, the long-time alpha male, Kamots, was overthrown.

Kamots was no spring chicken. He had held on to his position long past his prime by sheer force of personality. At some point though, personality is no longer enough.

After the revolution, everyone seemed to pick on the ousted leader. He was repeatedly thrashed as if grudges from previous years were being finally paid off. Several weeks later, Jeremy found what was left of Kamots in a corner of the compound. There wasn't much left at all.

Now began the struggle to become the new alpha. Two young males, Amani and Matsi, who had collaborated in Kamots's overthrow, were battling it out. Wound count in the pack mounted as the battle continued. Jeremy asked me to come for a medical inspection to see how bad things really were.

I couldn't do a proper inspection of all the animals from outside the fence. The wolves, unusually agitated, weren't coming close enough. Jeremy decided we should enter the compound. He was the real alpha. I was to stay close to him. If he decided it was unsafe, he would tell me to get out. When we got inside, we crouched low, in an appeasement posture, in hopes that the individual wolves would come over to inspect us while I inspected them. This worked well. They would hesitantly approach us, sniff us from several angles, perhaps even sniff our faces and give us a quick speculative lick. This was a bit nerve-wracking I must admit. I would have been just as happy if they had stopped a couple of strides away and quickly pirouhetted so I could inspect them from a safer distance. Matsi did just about exactly this. The only difference was that after he stopped, he looked me straight in the eye, then charged.

Even in a couple of strides, a 125-pound wolf can get up a fair head of steam. A crouching position is also not very stable. He bowled me over like I was a tenpin. I expected to feel him awarding me my very own omega patch.

But he didn't. Quickly Jeremy sprang to his feet and stepped between us. The real alpha male meant business. Matsi backed away. As I scrambled to my feet, I didn't need to be told it was time for me to get out. Matsi had asserted his dominance. I wasn't going to argue.

Not long after that, the struggle was suddenly over. Amani was the new alpha. Matsi was pretty beat up, half of his tail was gone. Now everyone else seemed to feel compelled to thrash the loser as well. This torment went on for several weeks until Matsi eventually found refuge in a tree, far from the site of most of the pack's activities.

In defeat, Matsi figured out a wonderful way to cope. Near the bottom of the compound, there was a dead snag that had half fallen over until it had wedged in the top of a living tree. In essence, it was a foot-wide ramp leading to a sheltered platform some twenty feet in the air. Matsi made it his new den. He grew wonderfully agile at springing up on the snag, turning quickly on it without losing his balance. As the only way to approach his refuge, it was easy to defend against wolves that might try to teeter up the ramp to attack him. He held the high ground. Intruders stood to fall a considerable distance. He was safe.

But Matsi couldn't spend all his time in the tree. He still had to come down to eat and drink. When he did, he was continually abused by the others. One day Jeremy phoned and said I had better come take a look at Matsi. He had what looked like a serious wound.

It looked serious enough to me. Someone had managed to rip open his scrotum and tear loose one of his testicles. It now dangled a full six inches below his scrotum, which itself was a bloody mess. I thought of the fact that he had previously had part of his tail bitten off. Usually a subordinate animal under attack will, like a dog, tuck its tail between its legs as it flees. Could this be why that behavior evolved? To protect the scrotum of a fleeing animal? Of course, females did it too. But I wasn't about to let an inconvenient fact interfere with my nice hypothesis. I'd see what Steve thought about it.

I didn't really offer advice. It was the board's job to make these decisions. I wasn't sure what might happen. I simply reported the possibilities. It was possible that Matsi's wound would heal just fine. The testicle and cord might eventually wither and just fall off. Wolves were very tough creatures. On the other hand, it could happen that the open scrotum would become infected, the infection could travel up into the abdomen and kill him from peritonitis.

The board decided that Matsi should be castrated. It was the safest medical decision. Then he was to be removed from the pack permanently for his own safety. He could live in the one-acre pen where we had operated on the females.

Jeremy had already isolated him in the pen when I arrived. Remembering our last interaction, I wasn't about to try to give him the anesthetic injection. Jeremy did it. The castration was routine, except that once when I accidentally banged some instruments together, Matsi suddenly lifted his head and stared directly at me just as I was snipping off a testicle. My stomach did a little flutter. Just as suddenly, his head flopped back down. I don't think he ever really woke up. The noise temporarily stimulated some ancient part of his brain. Taking no chances though, I gave him a boost of anesthetic before continuing.

In the weeks that followed, there was an amazing change in Matsi. He became a dog. A big, friendly, goofy dog. He licked me when I visited him and cavorted like a puppy soliciting play. He seemed to enjoy being patted. I was never completely at ease though. It was difficult to forget when he had flattened me so effortlessly. I also never knew whether he might suddenly remember me as the one he observed so calmly cutting off his testicles.

Dogs are not wolves, as I said, but they *were* wolves. Sometime during the past few thousands of years, we bred most of the wolf out of the dog. Most, but not all. Dominance issues may be muted a bit in dogs, but they are still there, and deserve attention. I pay attention. The wolves taught me to.

I pay attention to the dog's relationship with its owner. Is their dominance status clearly established? Owners need to be so securely established as the alpha, that there is never any testing. If the dog tends to test, then alpha status needs to be strongly reasserted. This means making the dog obey commands instantly, and punishing him for not responding immediately. It means not allowing the dog to put paws on its owner. It means paying attention to small details like making sure the owner goes through all doors ahead of the dog.

If the owner seems in firm control of the dog, I'll turn my attention to how it behaves toward children if they happen to be along. A good dog should not kowtow to the alpha, but bully everyone else. If I notice the animal pushes the children around or tried to separate them from their parent with its body, I'll point that out to the parent. Especially if it's still a puppy, I let the parent know that some professional obedience training is probably a wise precaution. If there are no children around, I'll see how the animal relates to me. Does it growl or threaten when I examine it? With small dogs and puppies, I'll sometimes flip them over on their backs to see how they respond to being dominated. If they become aggressive, it's another sign that trouble could lurk in the future. Again, professional obedience training is a good idea.

The pack dominance mentality is why bystanders are the ones who get hurt by aggressive animals. Domineering, aggressive owners often have aggressive dogs. This is no secret. The owner is the alpha, so the dog won't attack him. But the dog doesn't perceive himself to be the omega. He's the beta, therefore anyone besides his owner ranks below him, and is fair game for intimidation. So at first opportunity or perceived challenge, he bites the wife, the children, or the neighbor's wife or children. Then he's brought to me to be euthanized. I hate that. It doesn't have to be, if people paid attention to pack dynamics.

Steve's friend Jack was just this sort of owner. He didn't understand the lesson he should have learned after his wife had been mauled and maimed, which was that he was not observant enough to be trusted with potentially dangerous animals. He was large and fearless. He was always in control. What was the problem? Even worse, his pets, instead of being aggressive dogs, were aggressive lions. Lions are pack animals too. We call their packs prides.

After she was maimed, but before she divorced him, Dorothy's grown son Shawn came for a visit. Usually he avoided the odd family pets. He didn't enjoy being around them. They frankly scared him. Dorothy would ask Jack to put them in the garage until Shawn left. Usually he did so. But after the accident, Dorothy and Jack's relationship was rocky. They fought constantly anyway, and she didn't feel like another argument over the animals.

Jack made the lions lie down behind the couch and ordered them to stay. Shawn sat there nervously, pretending not to be alarmed by their proximity to his back. Before long, Rabbi, the big male, came swiftly over the couch's back, grabbed Shawn by the scalp and dragged him off into a corner. Jack dove into the pile and managed to free Shawn's head, ordering him to back out the door. Shawn was in no condition to obey. He was barely conscious. In shock, he just lay there bleeding. Rabbi grabbed him again, Jack freed him again. He screamed at Shawn not to be such a wimp, to get moving. Finally using the coffeetable as a bludgeon, he managed to back Rabbi into another room. Dorothy was screaming into the phone, the ambulance was on its way, the police not far behind.

Shawn did survive. He was badly scarred but alive, like his mother. Jack loaded the lions into his van and fled before the police got there. I never heard from him again, although I guess Dorothy did, because she told me several years later that they were now officially divorced. I did hear *about* Jack though. Several days after these events, he had stopped in at a wild animal exhibition park in the Bay area, where he tried to sell them his lions. They were well-trained, fine with seasoned trainers who weren't cowards, he told them. The park officials had already paid him for the lions, but Jack hadn't yet left the premises, when Rabbi went after one of the park's trainers. Jack saved that trainer too. A real Samaritan. While they waited for the ambulance to arrive, the officials told Jack the deal was off. They wanted their money back. Take his animals and take them fast. Jack drove away with his sociopathic animal family still intact, a sadder but probably not wiser man. He still didn't understand pack dynamics.

CHAPTER 16

Night Tales

Let's face it, strange things happen late at night. Sometimes these things are spooky, sometimes amusing in ways peculiar to the wee hours, sometimes just plain weird. When the phone rings during the day, you don't worry. When it rings at night, it makes sense to worry.

One of the reasons I ultimately decided I'd like to work in a university teaching hospital, as I do now, was to establish some reasonably normal working hours. Specifically, I wanted to get away from the nocturnal madness, the moronic inferno, as I had begun to think of it. Previously, I'd always worked until very late, or been on-call all night several times a week. The strangeness was finally getting to me. If you've ever seen the painting by Van Gogh called *The Night Café*, then you'll recognize how I felt. The colors are too bright, the lighting surreal, the atmosphere vaguely menacing. That's what being a night doctor is like.

I'm convinced John Barry was driven crazy by the night. He worked only nights—eleven to seven—your classic graveyard shift. Not a soul around except the technician up front to answer the door. In the back of the hospital where he liked to hide himself, there were just the sleeping or moaning animals, the silent gleaming floors, the ticking clock. I knew he had gone crazy when I saw what he did to Arlo.

Arlo was part coyote, I think—grayish, long-snouted, and lanky. Arlo also seemed to be terribly frightened all of the time. He was one of my first cases as a full-fledged and newly minted veterinarian. I was the new doc at a wonderful clinic in Albuquerque, New Mexico.

Steve had accepted a postdoctoral position at the University of New Mexico. So immediately after finishing vet school, I packed my car with my few belongings and my many pets and headed southwest from New York. Stopping once for minor car trouble, the mechanic stared at the jumble of cages, crates, and free ranging beasts in my backseat and asked if I owned a pet store.

Because New Mexico has no veterinary college, the Animal Care Clinic was quite probably the best veterinary hospital in the entire state, with six full-time doctors, amazingly up-to-date equipment, spacious facilities, twenty-four–hour service, and a serious commitment to provide the very best medical care. It had taken Dr. Tim Fitzpatrick, the owner, years of blood, sweat, and tears to build such a terrific hospital. I felt like I had been called up by the Yankees.

My guess is that I was hired because of my Cornell degree. Fitz was a Cornell graduate too. So were a couple of the other doctors. By hiring Cornell grads, Tim knew from firsthand experience they had had excellent training. First-rate training isn't necessarily enough to make a first-rate doctor, though. It remained to be determined whether I could put that training into practice. To be a good veterinarian, you need common sense, organizational skills, compassion, and not least—considerable people skills.

Most veterinary hospitals don't handle after-hour emergencies. They rely on specialized emergency clinics. If the ill or injured animal is still alive when its regular doctor comes to work the next morning, the regular doctor might take over the case if the animal is in any condition to be safely transported. Fitz didn't believe in using emergency clinics though. If a client were ours, he felt we owed it total care. Besides, he couldn't control the quality of the doctors hired by the local emergency clinic. He could control whom he hired.

Fitz had hired John Barry about a year previously to be his night doctor. Veterinarians willing to work graveyard are not all that easy to find. Barry, a small man with a laconic, somewhat wooden, personal manner, was also a Cornell grad. He didn't need to be coerced or cajoled into working graveyard. He wanted to do it. He seemed to enjoy the late night solitude. Also he wasn't always the most congenial doctor, which was not so much of a problem at night. He didn't actually need to meet that many people. Mostly he dealt with animals that had been admitted during the day and needed to stay overnight. Clients arriving with emergencies late at night were generally dealt with face-to-face by the technician-receptionist who was on with him.

When Arlo arrived late one afternoon, unconscious after being hit by a car, I thought he was a goner. He had taken the impact directly to the head. He had gruesome multiple fractures and lacerations of his head and face. A fractured sinus made his breathing visible on his forehead, where his skin rose and fell as he inhaled and exhaled. Other than the head trauma, he seemed pretty unscathed except for the expected scrapes and bruises. I started him on supportive care, which included intravenous mannitol which I hoped would suppress any brain-swelling. Pressure inside the skull is a major cause of death in head injuries. I sat with Arlo all night, making sure that the fluid mixture was changed exactly on time. Barry wandered through occasionally, scowling, but hadn't said a single word to me by the time I left around dawn. I needed to get some sleep before coming back to start my normal 10 A.M. shift.

By the time my day started, Arlo was not only alive, he was conscious, somewhat alert, and even felt well enough to try to bite me. I was ecstatic.

Arlo was what we call a fear-biter. Maybe he was part coyote after all. Coyotes are notorious fear-biters. He wasn't at all aggressive. He wouldn't go after you, but would back away, submissive but snarling, any time you approached. When he had backed himself into a corner and had nowhere else to retreat to, he would cower and snap if you pressed the issue. That was fine. I could deal with fear-biting.

The first thing I did was buy him a basket-muzzle, a sort of soft-wire cage that loosely covers the snout, at a nearby pet store. With the muzzle on, he couldn't bite and was even able to drink if he wanted to. I arranged for his owner, whom he wouldn't bite, to come in after he got off work, remove the muzzle long enough for Arlo to have a meal, then put it on again so he could be treated the rest of the night and day.

Arlo was going to need a long stay in the hospital, so I set about trying to become his friend. I hoped he would get over feeling threatened all the time. When I had a few spare minutes during the day, I would often go sit on the floor of his kennel and eat my lunch or write up hospital records. He'd back away and snap at me at first, but with the muzzle on I could ignore that. Eventually he would belly-crawl over and snuggle up to me as I wrote or ate. He even took bits of food from me through the muzzle, which sped up our bonding considerably.

He wasn't out of the woods yet, but a day later I had begun to feel fairly optimistic that he was going to make it. However, as a new doctor I was leaving nothing to chance. I was fanatical that all his treatments were done meticulously and exactly on time. Which is why I decided on the spur of the moment to go back in at 2 A.M. the second night he was with us to give him his scheduled injection myself. I wasn't asleep anyway—too keyed up after an exhausting day. Besides, Arlo had gotten somewhat used to me, so it might not be as traumatic for him to get a shot from someone he knew. With the broken bones in his face, I couldn't yet risk trying to give him oral medication. But I knew I could sit in his kennel, he would eventually crawl over to me, and I'd slip in his injection while distracting him with tasty morsels. That's how it worked during the day.

As I entered the kennel area, I heard what sounded like angry muttering followed by blood-chilling canine screams. Rushing to see what had happened, I found Barry in Arlo's kennel with his leash twisted around some bars to force him to the ground, one foot pressing his fractured face to the floor, about to slam home the injection like it was a spear.

I have a pretty unclear picture of what followed. I remember screaming—and I'm not a screamer—but I was screaming at Barry, sobbing, trembling with rage. I didn't physically assault him. Physical violence just isn't in me. But I badly wanted to. Even today, I get a knot in my stomach when thinking about it. How could anyone, much less a veterinarian, do such a thing?

I know I was screaming horrible threats, calling him every foul epithet I knew and some that I made up on the spot. Startled, he shouted right back, just as loud. This was *his* job, what was I doing here at this hour anyway, go home and go home now, he'll give injections any way he saw fit!

Whatever I said or did it must have made an impact, because I do remember that he ultimately disappeared to go on to his other treatments. I gave Arlo his injection. Then instead of returning home, I spent a long time sitting with him, sobbing quietly, trying to calm both of us down, thinking about what I would do next. My wonderful new job suddenly didn't look so wonderful anymore.

I was still red-eyed when Fitz arrived in the morning but I had my emotions under better control. I was no longer hysterical with rage. I was now coldly furious and resolute. I followed him into his office without asking. Before he had even taken off his coat, I said, "Either he goes or I go."

Poor Fitz, of course, had no idea who or what I was talking about. I described to the best of my recollection what had happened. I told him that I could understand incompetence, the world—including our profession—was rife with incompetence, maybe even indifference, but I could not stomach wanton cruelty. There was no excuse for it, ever. I could not work anyplace that would tolerate a doctor like Barry.

I fully expected that I would be the one to go. After all, I had just been there for a few weeks, Barry for a year. I was a brand new doc, as yet unskilled in many important ways. I certainly couldn't yet work with the speed and efficiency that bring in the real profits to a hospital. However, I was a conspicuously hard worker, and hoped it had been evident even during my short time there, that my clients meant everything to me.

Fitz didn't say anything for the longest time. He seemed lost in thought. I'm sure that he couldn't have imagined a much worse way to start his day. Finally, he asked didn't I have cases to treat? As I was walking out the door, I heard him phone the receptionist. "Get Dr. Barry on the phone, Donna. No, I don't care if he's still sleeping."

Fitz fired him the same day. It mustn't have been easy. He'd known Barry a lot longer than he'd known me. My guess is that he might have already had some suspicions about Barry. In any case, I've never ceased to admire him for what he did. He is a fine human being, and really was committed to humane pet care above all else. It wasn't just lip service. Just this year Fitz's daughter was admitted to Washington State Veterinary College where I now teach.

If she turns out to be half the doctor, or half the human being her father is, it will be a true delight to work with her in a few years when she passes through my service.

The immediate consequence of Barry's firing was that we no longer had a night doctor. Fitz decided to keep only a technician on for the night. We had a wonderful one, perfectly well qualified to follow treatment orders, assess patients' status, and phone a doctor if they seemed to be deteriorating. But it did mean that all of the doctors now had to be on-call some nights. On-call means being available at any time during the night to return telephone calls to clients with emergencies, and to go into the clinic to re-evaluate inpatients or receive animals that need immediate attention. No one complained about these new responsibilities, though. Not to me anyway.

If this weren't a "night" story, there would probably be nothing more to add. But there is more. I was now working the late shift most nights. The clinic officially closed at 9 P.M. After that, I had to treat any animals I'd taken in, and perform any urgent surgeries. Technically, I was supposed to finish by ten, but in reality I rarely left before midnight.

Within a few days of this new schedule, I began getting anonymous phone calls just before I closed up for the night. "I know where you live," a muffled voice would threaten. There were variations on this theme. "I know what time you leave." "The parking lot is dark, isn't it? Especially in the corner where you park your car." Of course, I recognized Barry's voice. One night I found a bunch of torn up photographs of nude women strewn inside my car. I thought about going to the police, but finally decided against it. Why bother? I had no proof. I was more careful to lock my car though. I tried pretty successfully not to feel frightened as well. He was too pathetic to fear, and this cowardly anonymous harassment was exactly the sort of thing I'd expect from someone who would satisfy his power fantasies on helpless injured animals.

I never responded to his taunts on the telephone either. No sense giving him the satisfaction. Eventually he got tired of his game. The phone calls stopped. Maybe he actually developed a life and didn't have the time for it anymore. Maybe he became a day person.

But other night people were still out there. And since I was so often at the clinic until midnight, I met more than my share of them. Anyone who phoned after nine had their call automatically forwarded to the answering service, which would relay the message and number of the caller to me at the clinic if I were still there, at home if I had already left. If the caller insisted that his pet needed to be seen immediately, I would tell him that I would be happy to see it, however I would have to charge an after-hour emergency fee to be paid upfront. If it was a real emergency, no one objected. If not, they found a way to put things off until morning. Only a few times did someone resent the emergency fee, and then only after I had determined their pet was in no danger. Then they occasionally decided that we were trying to gouge them for as much money as we could.

One group of three teenage boys, for instance, insisted that I see their kitten at 2 A.M. It wasn't really too sick, but the boys grew irritated and a bit abusive when I collected the emergency fee. Not long after they left I heard a series of crashes outside. I assumed it was a car wreck on the busy adjacent street—not an uncommon occurrence, but later when I left for home, I discovered that the wreck was with my car in the parking lot. The irate boys had apparently smashed their car into mine a number of times before leaving. I hoped that their vehicle looked as bad as mine did. This time I did phone the police, but it turned out that the address and phone number they had given me were phony. It figured.

The Baldwins probably would have done that to my car too, if they had thought of it. An elderly, deeply suspicious, thoroughly disagreeable couple with a lovely Persian cat named Princess Lela, the Baldwins had brought The Princess, pink rhinestone-studded collar and all, in for a routine vaccination. I happened to notice during her physical exam that her teeth and gums were in terrible shape. The possibility of oral abscesses spreading infection to the rest of the animal is a serious health hazard. When I recommended that their cat needed some dental work, they made no secret of their belief that I was simply trying to make as much money off them as possible. Few things are more irritating to me than this assumption. There may be doctors out there who do such things, but I pride myself on having never made a single medical decision in order to make more money. If anything, I do the reverse, undercharging people who seem to be financially strapped. If money were that important to me, I'd have gone into human medicine.

The Baldwins dithered. Would The Princess have to be anesthetized? Yes, I told them. Another cat of theirs had died under anesthesia years before, they told me. Could I assure them their cat wouldn't die? No, I told them, you can never guarantee that. Animals occasionally died from routine vaccinations too. The odds were very, very small though. We had come a long way with veterinary anesthesia in recent years. Finally, they agreed. The dental treatment went off routinely. I pulled a few teeth, scaled the others, cut away some damaged gums. Her mouth would be fine now. As they left, the Baldwins were still muttering about the cost and whether there was any real need for a cat to have dental work.

That night, I worked late, past midnight anyway. I had just got home, flopped on my couch to spend a few relaxing vegetative moments, probably scanning the pet section of the local newspaper when the phone rang. The Princess was flipping around the house with terrible uncontrollable seizures. They knew it would happen. That's what unnecessary medical procedures led to. What had they told me?

Rather than let them carry on with the I-told-you-so's while the cat possibly died, I interrupted to advise them to immediately wrap The Princess in heavy towels so she couldn't hurt herself or them. I'd meet them at the clinic as fast as we both could get there.

I lived about ten minutes away and arrived first. Wouldn't you know that these things happened with these sorts of clients? The ones who expected the worst, got the worst. I only hoped that I could somehow do something for the poor animal, even if I had to listen to the owners berate me while I worked. And in they came, the cat thrashing wildly inside the towel. It was all they could do not to drop the squirming bundle.

I advised the Baldwins to stand back while I carefully unwrapped the towel. The Princess immediately began flipping and thrashing wildly all right, but it wasn't the sort of completely uncontrollable thrashing you usually see in a classic grand mal seizure. There seemed to be a method to these convulsions, like when Elvis Presley sang *Jailhouse Rock*. I dropped the towel back over her, pinned her to the floor as best I could and carefully pealed part of the towel back to expose only her head and neck. Just as I thought. Reassuring her quietly as she still struggled beneath me, I slowly undid the pink rhinestone-studded collar. Her left front leg had somehow managed to slip inside the collar. It had been pinned alongside her head. She had panicked.

I handed the collar to Mr. Baldwin. Then I handed him the towel. We wouldn't be needing it anymore. Princess Lela lay on the floor, exhausted from her struggles. Finally she sat up and began licking her paws. I scratched her neck. She purred. Without so much as a "Thank you" or "We're sorry," the Baldwin's picked her up and headed for the door.

"One moment, folks," I said. "That will be $65 for the emergency fee. There's no charge for the treatment."

If they had been more pleasant folks, I probably would have waived the emergency fee. But sometimes you just can't help yourself. They got no break.

The Dude and Hugo got no break either. It wouldn't have been fair to Max, their monster pitbull. Of course, it was a night case too. They rolled into the parking lot in one of those high-rider pickups—the kind that are jacked up so high it looks like you need a ladder to reach the door handle. It was about eleven. I was just getting into my car, ready to head home.

The driver vaulted from his seat. He might have been five feet tall in thick-soled boots. I was curious how he got into his truck in the first place. He was a dude, though. A real *cholo*, as we said in Albuquerque. He had the clothes, the hair, the attitude. "Hey, man, are you the doctor?" He was helping his girlfriend down from the cab. Two other friends, another couple, were descending without ropes from the other side of the truck.

"Yes, I'm Dr. K. What can I do for you?"

"It's Max. He's hurt real bad. We were hoping you could fix him, man. Want me to bring him inside?"

I wasn't sure. They reeked of whisky and the men, at least, were very obviously drunk. I didn't know if Max was a parakeet, a cat, or a horse. I wasn't even sure there was a Max. We had enough controlled drugs in the hospital to make several fortunes on the street. I had to be careful. Also, sometimes you need to be careful moving an injured animal. I thought I'd rather stay outside in the parking lot, where passing cars could see us at least until I figured out what Max's problem was.

"Maybe I should take a look at Max out here first. Where is he, and what happened to him?"

"He's in the truck, man. Where do you think he is?

And well, man, we're not exactly sure what happened to him." At this The Dude's girlfriend hissed something to him in Spanish and he started over. "Okay, what I meant was we had a little accident. See we were partying and chained Max to the bumper, man, so he wouldn't get lost or some shit like that. You know how partying goes, man. When we left, we forgot about Max. Daniella here remembered about him just after we got on the freeway, man. He was in pretty rough shape by then."

I was trying to get my mind around what I was hearing. "Are you telling me that you dragged Max behind your truck? Down city streets and onto the freeway? Jesus," I couldn't help myself, "and he's still alive?"

"I think so, man. In rough shape, though. Let's see how he's doing. Hey Hugo, man, give me a hand." He scrambled into the back of his pickup with the impressive ease of a leopard slithering up a tree. "Max, man, how you doing? I've seen you look better, man." He and Hugo proceeded to haul down the biggest pitbull I've ever seen. His head looked as big as a lion's. He weighed at least eighty pounds, and fifty of that must have been head. The rest of him was a mess. So far as I could tell in the dim parking lot light, he was alive though. It was easy to see him breathing. He had virtually no fur and no skin left on his chest, belly, or one whole side.

They did have a real medical problem. I asked them bring Max inside where I could get a better look. Max was probably a fighting dog. There were lots of illegal dogfights in New Mexico and lots of dogs, mostly pitbulls, were bred to fight in them. I treated the survivors fairly frequently. They were wonderful dogs to work on. Ask any veterinarian and she will tell you that pitbulls make marvelous patients and marvelous pets. They are calm, affectionate, and stoic, probably from the incredible pain threshold that has been bred into them. A pitbull is not going to fear-bite and it is not going to attack your child because she accidentally twisted its ear too hard.

Unfortunately, a lot of sick people buy pitbulls and spend all their energy trying to train them to be vicious. Making them aggressive toward other aggressive dogs doesn't take much effort, but even those dogs are usually lovely around people. Sometimes, however, with enough effort, slob owners can turn a nice animal into a vicious attack dog, and when this happens because of their muscularity and phenomenal jaw strength, you have a really dangerous animal. Those sorts of animals are pretty rare, though, at least in my experience.

Max's injuries were as bad as I had suspected. The first thing he needed was some serious pain medication. I couldn't really believe that he hadn't gone berserk from pain while being carried, but that's a pitbull for you. If Max pulled through at all, it was going to mean a week or even more in the hospital, some skin grafting, lots and lots of treatment. Lots and lots of money. I gave Max the strongest pain relief, oxymorphone, we had, then turned to get a few things settled with The Dude and his friends.

"Look, all of you, if Max makes it at all, he is going to require a lot of treatment. I'll need an emergency fee, and a deposit on his treatment, up front. Right now, that is. Otherwise, I can't help him. By tomorrow evening, I'll probably have a better idea of how much it might cost altogether. Give me a call, or stop by then, if you decide to leave him."

The four of them discussed the situation in Spanish. They spoke much too fast for me to have any idea what they were saying. I got the idea that the guys would have been happy to take him home and hope for the best. But the women were not having any of it. One of them kept snapping her fingers and holding out her hand for Hugo's wallet. They managed to scrape together about $100 between the four of them. That was enough. I told them I had better get to work on Max. They could phone in the morning to see how he was doing. As they left, the guys were nudging each other and giggling. I think they thought the whole situation was pretty amusing. The women kept a stony silence even as they were being hoisted back aboard the truck. I resolved that if I did manage to save Max, he wasn't going back to Hugo and The Dude.

I couldn't do a lot with him that night. I started him on fluids, cleaned up the worst of his wounds, loaded him up on antibiotics and some short-acting steroids. By the next morning, he was doing much better. He even ate a bit. I decided he was now more likely to survive anesthesia, so I knocked him out, castrated him (his testicles and scrotum had been scraped into near oblivion), cleaned and sutured the few wounds where there was enough skin left to pull together. Over the next few days, Max continued to improve. We jury-rigged a whirlpool bath from one of our standard grooming tubs, so that we could wash away the dead cells and gooey exudate which accumulates on injuries like these, inhibiting healing. Max grew very close to Jan, the technician who gave him these whirlpools. He would lay his massive head on her shoulder while she patiently went over each inch of his flayed body, gently cleaning him. I could see Jan bonding to Max too as the days passed. I was beginning to formulate a plan.

Someone, not The Dude himself but probably his girlfriend, phoned nearly every day to see how Max was doing. After about day five, I spoke with whomever it was that had been calling. I said that the bill was now $2,500 and would probably be in the neighborhood of $4,000 when he was ready to go home. If he had had responsible owners, Max could probably have gone home then. But I didn't trust them to treat Max at home, so I was making sure he stayed with us. The Dude now came to the phone in a hurry. "Four grand, man, are you serious? This is robbery, man. Why don't you just stick a gun in my face?"

"I'm sorry you feel that way. But medical services can be quite expensive. Max will probably be able to go home in about a week. That should give you enough time to get the payment together."

As the time for Max's release came closer, The Dude asked about a payment plan. This was reasonable and something we usually arranged. However I was adamant that Max was not going back to someone who would drag him behind a truck and then giggle about it later. No deal, I said. It had to be payment-in-full or we couldn't release Max.

The Dude put on a good show for his girlfriend. He threatened lawsuits and lawyers. He threatened to come down and settle things himself. He threatened whatever he could think of. When I didn't respond, he came up with his cleverest idea.

"Okay, doc, what about instead of *me* being out four grand, *you* be out four grand? How does that sound, man? You know what? You just bought yourself a $4,000 dog. Have a nice day." He slammed the phone down.

My plan had worked. I asked Jan if she would take care of an abandoned dog just for a few weeks while we tried to find him a home. As time passed, I did his skin grafts. The grafts bonded well. Jan and Max bonded well too. Eventually he was as good as new. He now had a better owner, though.

Sometimes, it wasn't the type of calls or the night-owl clientelle that made night work so unpredictable. It was just that you were up late at night when everyone is on edge.

I've always made house calls. I don't do it routinely, but if I have a particularly elderly or disabled client, I'll happily go by his house to treat his animal on my way to work or my way home. If I got out of the clinic at ten or eleven though, this meant knocking on someone's door fairly late at night, which isn't a problem if they expect you. I always phoned before I called. Imagine my surprise one night then, when they wouldn't let me in.

I had phoned Maria before I left. It was probably a little after ten, not late by my standards. Her cat had cancer and was on a chemotherapy regime. Maria had recently broken her hip and had trouble getting around. I decided it would save her a lot of trouble if I did the chemo treatment at her home. It would be no doubt less traumatic for the cat too.

Chemotherapeutic drugs are nothing to fool around with. They are potentially very toxic and need to be handled with exceptional caution. Moreover, OSHA has created a labyrinth of rules for handling these drugs, which is as rigorous as it is impenetrable. If an animal on chemotherapy urinates in an uncontrolled area, for instance, we have to clean up the urine with all the precautions you might take with plutonium or anthrax.

So when I set off for Maria's, my car was packed with all the required gear. Parking in front of her house, I donned a surgical gown and chemo mask, which is kind of like a normal surgical mask on steroids. I put on my chemo booties, my large chemo gloves, and my face shield. I now looked like I was ready to explore the moon or battle a riotous crowd. Carrying the drug itself, vincristine, in a special plastic chemo bag the size of a small pillowcase marked CAUTION BIOHAZARD in large red letters, I banged on the door, ready to crack a joke about my appearance.

Nothing happened for a while. The door didn't open. No porch light came on. Finally, a small voice croaked, "Go away."

"Maria, it's me, Dr. K. I've got Percy's chemo. Open up before I get arrested for impersonating a spaceman."

"Go away. Git. I'll call the police. You *will* get arrested all right," the voice now sounded a bit scared. Was Maria joking? Had she been drinking? Maybe with all the gear on she didn't she recognize me.

I lifted my face shield so she could see me better and tried once more, "Maria! Mrs. Archuleta. It's me, Dr. K. Remember I phoned just a few minutes ago? I'd like to give Percy her shot, so I can go home and get some sleep. Please, open up."

There was a few seconds silence before the voice croaked once again, angrily this time. "I said go—now—and don't come back. If you're not off my porch in five seconds, I'm calling the police. Go right now. And Maria Archuleta, if that's who you really want, lives across the street."

I did have my own problems with the police later that week. But they had nothing to do with frightening defenseless little ladies. This time I apparently frightened a strapping young man.

The evening had been a catastrophe. Just before closing a boxer had come in whose stomach had exploded. This occasionally happens, particularly with big dogs like Great Danes and St. Bernards. For reasons that no one really understand, the stomach becomes twisted around itself, gas builds up inside, and eventually the stomach will explode. When that happens, the dog dies. Period. If it doesn't die immediately from blood loss, it dies soon after from infection—peritonitis. That's what we learned in vet school.

But this boxer's owners were adamantly against my suggestion to euthanize it. Wasn't there something I could try, no matter how small the chance? These were people after my own heart. I told them I could promise nothing, their dog would almost certainly die, but I would do what

I could. This is the sort of thing you do when you are a new doc. You don't admit when things are hopeless.

I spent the next four or five hours working on the animal. I opened her up—she was bleeding profusely—and slaved among the blood, guts, and gore. I cut, cleaned, and sutured. I used gallons and gallons of sterile solution to try to rinse her insides as clean as possible. "The solution to pollution is dilution," as I learned in vet school. That was the only way I might possibly prevent peritonitis. I installed a number of fancy drains, so that I could continue to rinse her insides the next day. Amazingly enough, she not only pulled through the surgery that night, but ultimately fully recovered. I've never been that fortunate again since. I didn't realize then how lucky the boxer and I had been.

I wasn't so lucky on the drive home. I was completely exhausted and there was no exultation that the boxer was still alive because I fully expected to find her dead in the morning. It was now 3 A.M. and I was facing a thirty-five minute drive home. Steve and I had recently moved. We were now living among the junipers and pinyon pines in the Sandia mountains just east of town. Two clients of mine had abruptly moved back to the east coast. They needed housesitters until their New Mexico home sold. We leapt at the chance to get out of the city. But now it took me a lot longer to drive to and from the clinic. That was the price that country life extracted.

Instead of showering and changing from my surgical scrubs, now covered with so much blood and bits of tissue that I looked like I'd probably been butchering cattle all day, I decided to drive home as I was. I would shower and change there. I spread some plastic garbage bags to protect my carseat.

I know I shouldn't have been speeding, but was too tired to notice. I saw the parked squad car and radar gun as I passed, but it didn't register. At 3 A.M., after what I'd just been through, a lot of things didn't register.

When a police officer suddenly pulls in the darkened street in front of you at 3 A.M. and motions you to pull over and stop, it's usually alarming enough. However as it suddenly dawned on me what I must look like, it was even more alarming than usual.

He approached the car cautiously with one of those monstrous police flashlights glaring in my face. I couldn't see exactly when he drew his revolver, but remember him telling me to step away from the car very slowly keeping my hands where he could see them at all times. He spread-eagled me against my car while he called for backup. Then he frisked me, searching apparently for my bloody cleaver.

Thank goodness at that time none of my usual clients were likely to drive by. I spent more than an hour locked in the back of the squad car while the police ran every check they could think of on me. My explanations about having just finished five hours of arduous surgery on a dog with a ruptured stomach seemed to make no impression. They must have been contacting the morgue to see if any dismembered bodies had come in.

By the time I finally got home, it was beginning to get light. Now I was too tired to even shower. I dropped my scrubs on the floor and fell into bed. Steve would awaken first in the morning, but he would understand.

The most difficult thing about being on-call was not the long hours. I'd worked long hours in vet school. The most difficult thing was being awakened from the deepest sleep, needing to forget about what you were dreaming, and gather your wits quickly enough to phone back the client with some sensible questions to ask. You had to make a quick, reasonable judgment about whether you needed to see the animal immediately or whether it could wait until the clinic opened in the morning. With practice, I eventually got so that I was awake and alert almost instantly when the phone rang. If it turned out that I didn't have to go in to the hospital, I developed the capacity to almost as quickly fall back into a deep sleep.

Of course, calls after midnight are nothing like calls during the day, so even more night strangeness began to creep into my life. Sometimes it was just the nature of the phone calls themselves. People are more often chemically impaired at night, and even the ones who aren't just don't seem as coherent. The answering service would sometimes try to brace me for a particularly strange one when they phoned. "Dr. K, sorry to wake you, but we've got a guy who says his snake suddenly turned schizophrenic. Do you want to get back to him?"

I would invariably phone them back, no matter how strange it seemed. The one you didn't call would turn out to be real crisis and you'd regret it ever after. A few of the calls you can't help but remember.

"Hello? Mr. Lewis? This is Dr. K. from the Animal Care Clinic. I understand that you have a sick snake? Can you describe his symptoms to me?"

"Well, doc, it's the dangedest thing. He's got bugs."

"Bugs?"

"That's right, bugs. I been watching 'em. They're tiny, but I got me a magnifying glass, and I seen 'em crawl right through his skin. He's got thousands of 'em."

I thought I recognized the problem. "How big are these bugs, Mr. Lewis? About the size of a sesame seed? And flat? Very flat?"

"A what kind of seed? Naw, they're about as big as a booger. And flat, whoa yeah, I'll say, flatter than a flapjack."

That's what I thought. "Your snake has scale mites, Mr. Lewis. They're not a danger. You can either bathe it with Ivory soap or bring it in to us during regular business hours and let us do it. Good night, Mr. Lewis."

"Wait a second, Doc. I said my snake has bugs all over him. I don't know about any scale whatevers, these are bugs. You got to help me, Doc."

"Scale *mites*, Mr. Lewis. Mites, like small ticks. Yes, small bugs, if you wish, but they pose no health problem. If you bathe your snake with Ivory soap, or bring it..."

"Doc, I don't need a bath. I said my snake has bugs, thousands of 'em and sometimes they just disappear. There. There goes one now. He's gone. I tell you, you got to help me."

After enough time, I would eventually say goodnight and hang up even if I hadn't got my message across. I figured those callers wouldn't remember calling in the morning anyway.

I didn't mind going in to the hospital late at night if I had to. That was part of the job. But I wasn't about to go in again to meet Mr. Gallegos. He had pushed me beyond my limit. Mr. Gallegos phoned me first a few days before—at about 3 A.M. His terrier, Perrito, was having stomach problems, vomiting, and diarrhea. I had to see him now.

After discovering that Perrito had only vomited once so far—at about midnight—and that the diarrhea was what prompted the phone call, I assured Mr. Gallegos that considering it was 3 A.M. now, Perrito would probably survive the four hours until the clinic opened. In the meantime, he might want to make sure that Perrito didn't eat anything more. And if he had a room with an easily cleanable linoleum or tile floor, like a bathroom, he might want to lock him in that room in case the diarrhea persisted. If he weren't better by morning, one of our doctors would be able to see him right away.

No, no, he needed to be seen by someone now. If Perrito died during the night it would be my fault. Wasn't it my job to see animals that needed treatment? Poor Perrito.

He was right. I was supposed to see the client if they insisted. I advised him about the emergency fee, dressed quickly, and sped to the clinic. I didn't know exactly where Mr. Gallegos lived, but I could tell from his telephone prefix that it wasn't far away. Still he wasn't there when I arrived thirty-five minutes later. And he still wasn't there an hour after that when I finally gave up and drove back home. In fact, he never brought Perrito in the next day or anytime after. Some people don't seem to appreciate the value of other people's sleep.

I'm not easily riled, but I had to do something.

The phone must have rung at least a dozen times before it was answered, groggily. A man's voice. Good. I was hoping I wouldn't get the wife, if (poor lady) there were one.

"Mr. Gallegos?"

"Whaa? Is this...? Who did you...? What time is it?"

"Ah, Mr. Gallegos, it *is* you. Good. It's a little after three. I'm glad you're awake too. I hate it when I can't sleep and there's no one else to talk to. This is Dr. K, the veterinarian. Remember me? I'm phoning to see how Perrito is doing. Have those pesky stomach problems gotten any better?"

"Perrito? Veterin...? Hunh? Stomach?" He didn't seem to be fully awake yet. Then, after a pause and some rustling around. "After three? Did you say AFTER THREE? IT'S THE MIDDLE OF THE !#@$%#&%@#! NIGHT!" Now he was awake. For some reason, he didn't seem all that happy to hear from me. There was a crash. The line went dead. Mr. Gallegos, it seemed, had hung up on me.

Over the course of the following weeks whenever I was awakened by my emergency service in the middle of night, I always made it a point to phone Mr. Gallegos before going back to sleep. I was pretty sure that he wanted to be awake just as much as I did. After the first call, I realized that I had better not identify myself. There must be a law against such things. In fact, I didn't have to say a word. I'd just let the phone ring until Mr. Gallegos answered. Then, I would very gently hang up and fall back to sleep the sleep of the blessed.

CHAPTER 17

Guns

I've always been vaguely uncomfortable around guns. Growing up in rural Columbia County, New York, I lived far enough from New York City and Albany for there to be plenty of corn-fed deer in the local woods and fields, yet close enough to these cities to experience hoards of intent but inexperienced hunters descending on the area each fall when deer season opened.

They were easy to spot, the city folk, with their freshly starched and ironed cotton camos, shiny new boots, spotless blaze-orange caps and vests. You saw them stalking the field edges in twos and threes, gripping their rifles like briefcases, the barrels directed casually at the buttocks of their hunt-buddy in front of them. My neighbors, mostly dairy farmers, took hunting season very seriously. It was a fall ritual for them to spend afternoons spray-painting their black-and-white Holstein cattle with the word "COW!" in large Day-Glo orange letters. We always made sure to keep the dogs inside during hunting season too. One local legend had it that a proud fellow with a city accent pulled into a state hunt check station displaying his permit prominently on the leg of the German shepherd carcass he had stretched across his hood. Who knows whether that story was apocryphal or not? It shows pretty clearly the local attitude toward city hunters.

I come by my fear of guns honestly. My mother doesn't like them either. She was raised around hunters—competent hunters, who identified their target before they shot and generally hit what they were shooting at. Her father, Walter, ran a hunting lodge in the Adirondacks. Walter was born in Russia, immigrating to the U.S. just before World War I. After years of odd jobs, saving his money, he bought the lodge and hired expert deer hunters and trackers from the Old Country. He developed a clientele of wealthy city folks who would journey up to the lodge each season to drink and tell tall tales among the spruce and the firs. If it didn't interfere too much with their drinking, they might even venture into the forest occasionally and fire off an odd shot here and there. Walter's trackers would lead them to the deer and point them in approximately the right direction. If that weren't help enough, the trackers would shoot the deer themselves, then congratulate the clients on their remarkable aim and grace under pressure. When the clients sobered up, they might even have believed it.

Walter did all right for himself. When he died, my mother inherited a veritable armory of weapons that he had acquired over the years. Having heard her father's stories about drunken city hunters all her life, she wanted nothing to do with guns. She took the lot of them to the nearest gun shop, accepting the first price they offered.

As I got older, nothing happened to force a change in my attitude toward guns. Each year, it seemed one of my schoolmates was injured or killed in a hunting accident. After I began working in my first veterinary hospital, I saw firsthand the horrible toll guns took on pets and livestock. In my imagination, what went on in the human hospitals was even worse. So far as I could tell, when someone picked up a gun their IQ immediately dropped at least fifty points. I didn't know many people who could afford a drop like that.

So when I moved out West for the first time—to Albuquerque—I was more than a little alarmed to find that guns were as common as car keys. It wasn't just hunters carrying rifles in the forest, everyone everywhere seemed armed to the teeth. Restaurants had signs behind the cash registers warning customers to leave their guns outside. The traffic accidents reported in the newspaper always seemed to turn into roadside shootouts. At our neighborhood liquor store, Kelly's, everyone carried a pistol—the cashiers, the shelf stockers, the janitors. There were closed-circuit video cameras monitoring every corner of the store. I wondered whether I might be gunned down sometime when reaching suddenly for my handkerchief if struck by a sneezing attack while shopping. This particular store even had an armed employee patrolling the parking lot. The first time we stopped there, Steve thought we were about to be carjacked.

But guns were good for business at the animal hospital. Like clockwork, on Friday and Saturday nights, the maimed and mutilated would start arriving. The number of bullet-shattered limbs I treated even helped make me a better orthopedic surgeon. The main thing I learned was not to be too invasive. A seriously shattered bone is nearly impossible to piece back together with plates and screws. Usually when you try to do it, you compromise the local blood supply so much that things never heal. I found that I had the best success with external fixaters, fragment stabilizers that form a frame outside the skin. If you fix the big pieces of bone in place, it is remarkable how well nature will fill in the rest.

My gun phobia gradually crept to the back of my mind as the months passed. Constant exposure was inuring me to them. Life was also very good. After firing Dr. Barry, Fitz, with his genius for creating a productive medical environment, had turned the hospital into something as close to one big happy family as I could imagine.

The doctors were an eccentric but talented group. Veterinary medicine wasn't necessarily their whole life, like it was mine, but they were all highly competent professionals.

Dr. C.'s specialty was internal medicine. She didn't much like to do surgery, but would if she had to. I liked surgery, so we made an arrangement where I took some of her surgery cases, while she helped pick up the slack in my nonsurgical cases. I still run into her at professional meetings occasionally.

I still run into Dr. G. too. His major goal in life was to get on the television quiz show *Jeopardy!*. Veterinary medicine was only a means to provide a comfortable life while he studied for the show. He moved a television into the doctors' office space and scheduled his breaks around the show. His desk was piled high with books on *Jeopardy!*—

answers, questions, facts, and its history. He flew to Los Angeles several times to try out as a contestant. He wasn't at all discouraged when he failed to be invited back, he just ordered more books of *Jeopardy!* questions and answers, and watched even more religiously, trying to discern the stage personality he would need to develop in order to be chosen next time.

Dr. B. was out to make money—period. Fitz paid us, if we wanted, a percentage of the money we brought into the practice. It made good motivational sense. The harder you worked, the more money you could make. He didn't offer that option to doctors until they had worked for him long enough that he was sure that this incentive would not compromise their medical judgment.

It certainly made Dr. B. work hard. It made him pretty creative with his charges as well. He had a hard-edged, sarcastic sense of humor, which he hid well from the clients. To them, he seemed to come across as a favorite nephew. In the back room, he was Dennis the Menace. I noticed extra charges on some of his bills which were annoted "AG-$10." I pointed out to him that we already had a check box on the form for "anal gland" expression. "That's not 'anal gland,'" he grinned at me, "that's 'aggravation.'" Fitz figured that one out pretty quickly and put an end to it. Not before Dr. B. had made a tidy sum though.

Dr. B. also put up a MAC list on the wall of the doctors' office, MAC meaning "most annoying client." Each doctor could vote for his or her favorite candidate and at the end of the year we would toast the winner.

There was also a wonderful egalitarianism among the staff. There were probably a dozen technicians, of several grades of pay and medical sophistication. But there was no jealously or backbiting among them about pay or status. Fitz wouldn't tolerate it. The head tech was Mindy. She had been there for years and consequently got the most desirable shift—7 A.M. to 3 P.M. Besides being a wonderful tech, capable of doing three jobs simultaneously and doing them all well, she helped teach the newer techs specific skills. She also set up their work schedules, ordered supplies, and dealt with the personality conflicts that occasionally arose. She was a real Westerner, stout and muscular, always arriving at the office in cowboy hat and boots, large leather shoulder bag, and silver belt buckle the size of a saucer. She won the belt buckles in barrel racing competitions at rodeos around the state. Very occasionally, when we happened to get off work at the same time, she'd invite me over for dinner if she knew Steve was out of town. Her mother and father were usually there, as was her husband, Frank, a welder who aspired to be a policeman.

Of the half dozen or so receptionists, my favorite was Rhonda. Rhonda's life was her religion, or maybe the other way around. Religious feelings were never part of my nature or upbringing. In fact, if such feelings are worn too obtrusively on someone's sleeve, it generally puts me off. There seems to me to be a niggling sort of moral one-upmanship about it. But Rhonda wasn't like that. She was simply sweet, quietly pious. A smiling, always good-natured receptionist, she inevitably found a good side to our clients, no matter how troublesome they might be to the doctors. She could also absorb the wrath of the most irate clients, never lose her smile, and hopefully make them feel a little guilty about their tantrum even before they got out the door. *Zaftig*, with curly blond hair, pale, almost translucent skin, and bright red lipstick, she made Pollyanna look like a grouch.

One time I saw Rhonda waiting for a bus as I got off work and offered her a ride home. I discovered that she, her husband, Clint, and their four young children lived in a small trailer at the local KOA campground. Clint had short brown hair with a toothbrush moustache. He was unemployed, spending his days caring for the house and children or going door-to-door proselytizing their religion. They were in Albuquerque, Clint told me, because God had called them there. They lived entirely on Rhonda's receptionist's income. She took care of all practical details of their life, bought the groceries, paid the bills, planned for the future. Clint was focused on a higher calling.

To build and maintain the hospital *espirit de corp* Fitz put together, and paid for, lots of group activities. Each year, we had a Christmas party, spouses and family invited, at one of Albuquerque's finest restaurants. There was also a summer barbeque, usually at Fitz's house. We even had a well-publicized mock dog show for our clients. This was sponsored by a local radio station and pet store. There were contests for "fastest tailwag," "most aloof cat," "best pet and owner costume," "lowest ground clearance," and "pet that looked most like owner." The hospital staff judged the events. Our clients loved it. So did we.

Often a bunch of us would eat lunch together, the doctors, the techs, and the receptionists. We really enjoyed one another's company. We'd occasionally go out for drinks after work or have one another over for dinner.

If I've always been vaguely uncomfortable around guns earlier in life, I'm worse now. I allow no guns of any kind, even toy ones, inside my house. I think all hunting rifles ought to be registered, bullets locked in separate cabinets from the guns themselves, and ownership rights linked to training and psychological testing. Handguns should be illegal. Period. This is pretty much the way it is done in England. I've never told anyone the full story of why I feel this way. Not even Steve knows about it in detail. Fifteen years after the event, I think I'm up finally up to going back over the events of that day in March.

That winter, things just seemed to turn sour. If I were astrologically inclined, I'd say the stars were in a bad alignment. If I were religiously inclined, I'd say someone had been sinning, big time.

First, we had a dog inexplicably disappear from the hospital. Its owner left it to board while he was out of town, and one day it was gone. No one had the slightest idea whether it had somehow escaped, or had been stolen, or how either might have happened. The owner, needless to say, was furious, even after the dog was found unharmed. We were all very disturbed about it.

Then I walked into the studio to do my radio show one day and found the producer on the floor, unconscious in a pool of blood. I'd been doing a once a week radio call-in show at KZIA for months. It had gotten pretty routine until now. I phoned 911. When the ambulance arrived, my producer had revived. Had he been shot? Mugged? No, it seems he had been tilting his chair back, too far as it turned out, focusing his attention on the music in his headset, when his chair tumbled over backwards. The floor was concrete. He couldn't get his hands up in time to break his fall. He had a nasty concussion.

Then Dr. B. was nearly killed by a lead plumbing pipe the size of a baseball bat, which crashed through the hospital ceiling one day out of nowhere. The pipe had apparently been left leaning against a rafter by the construction crew that had installed our dropdown ceiling several years before. A slammed door finally dislodged it. It struck Dr. B. only a glancing blow on the head. It smashed our blood chemistry analyzer to bits.

Incredibly, he survived without permanent damage. It did our hospital permanent damage though, because Dahlia, a technician with a long-time crush on him, volunteered to take Dr. B. to the emergency room. When he was released from the hospital, she volunteered to take him home to make sure he was really all right. Six weeks later, she announced she was pregnant by Dr. B. He denied responsibility. When court-ordered blood tests revealed that he was indeed the father, he claimed that Dahlia had taken advantage of him in his weakened state. Dahlia, one of our best techs, could not go on working with him. She quit, and the rest of the techs didn't easily forgive him for it. The hospital no longer seemed like quite such a big happy family.

Then there was the citywide trauma of the Linda Lee Daniels case. Linda Lee was a pretty student at the University of New Mexico, who one day decided to make a quick run to the supermarket and never returned. It turned out that she had been abducted in broad daylight from the parking lot of a shopping center not far from our hospital. Several days later, her naked body was found in an arroyo outside town. She had been raped, strangled, and shot.

Some crimes seem to put a whole city on edge. This was one of those crimes. The victim was seemingly chosen completely at random. The murder was particularly brutal. She was not prowling a crime-infested neighborhood at the time. She was innocently shopping in a good part of town. Plus she was abducted in broad daylight from a crowded parking lot of a major shopping center that virtually everyone I knew shopped at regularly. It could have been any of us.

Women at the hospital were particularly concerned. The shopping center was close by. Many of the employees left by themselves after dark. Most of our parking lot could not be seen by passers-by on the street. It became a habit for the techs and receptionists to do everything in small groups.

One Friday in March, I was performing some minor surgery in one of our procedure rooms when Mindy and Rhonda ambled through asking if I'd like to accompany them to lunch. I'd had an exhausting week. Fitz was out of town, and I was covering his normal daytime hours plus working nights. I logged 120 hours that week, the most I'd ever worked. I thanked them, but said no I just wanted to finish up appointments and go home to sleep.

As they gathered their coats and purses from the adjacent storage room, I hear a small pop, no louder than a champagne cork. A few moments later, someone shouted, "Oh my God," with enough urgency that I rushed into the room to see what had happened.

Rhonda looked confused. Blood was spreading on the front of her blouse. Mindy seemed strickened too. I wasn't sure who might fall over first. We all just stared at one another for a moment. "She's been shot," Mindy finally choked.

I led Rhonda gently back into the procedure room. She was bleeding from a wound on her back too. Behind my hand, I whispered, "Nine-one-one NOW! RIGHT NOW!" to the stunned techs who had been helping me. I suggested to Rhonda she should probably lie down. She was beginning to collapse anyway. We made a pillow out of towels.

Word spread quickly through the hospital that Rhonda had been shot. A waiting client happened to be an emergency medical technician, a night worker on the local ambulance service. I never did learn his name. He rushed into the room and helped me do what we could for her. By the time the ambulance crew arrived, incredibly quickly, we had put pads over her wounds, got an IV catheter in place, and started her on fluids. She now looked even paler than normal.

The ambulance crew knew my helper. He filled the crew in on what he knew, as I held Rhonda's hand and tried to keep her talking. It helped me, and I hoped her, keep a reassuring grip on sense and sanity. Did she know where she was? Yes. Did she know who I was? Yes. You're

Dr. K. What a silly question. Everything was going to be all right, I assured her. She didn't answer.

The ambulance crew was outstandingly professional. They dealt with gunshot wounds a lot. They quickly put pressure cuffs on her legs, started her on oxygen, and loaded her into the ambulance. I still hadn't let go of her hand. "Can I come along?" I asked. I sat next to her in the ambulance and continued to hold her hand all the way to the hospital.

It wasn't until I was in the ambulance that I had a chance to go back in my mind over what had happened, to try to make some sense out of how someone standing in a backroom of a hospital could be shot. Mindy had apparently had a gun in her purse. I later found out that she had been carrying a Derringer ever since the Linda Lee Daniels abduction. The safety was not properly set. Her purse had banged against an oxygen tank in the storage room as she turned to pick up her coat. The gun had fired.

Rhonda now looked frightened. "Am I going to die?" No, you'll be fine. Don't worry. These fellows have the situation under control. I wasn't sure if I believed myself or not. Rhonda wasn't fooled. "K, please you've got to promise me...tell Clint good-bye. Please. Tell him I love him. Tell him to kiss the children for me. And don't let him forget that Mary is allergic to strawberries. He needs to remember that. She gets terrible hives. Tell him..." She seemed to lose her train of thought. I couldn't say anything. I just nodded.

She was still semiconscious in the emergency room. I stood in a corner while the doctors worked furiously over her. They rammed chest tubes into her, trying unsuccessfully to deaden the pain as they did so. She screamed again and again and again. I covered my ears, wincing with each scream, trying to will myself into a universe without pain, without screaming, without guns.

As they prepped her for surgery, I found some scrubs piled on a table. I put them on and followed them into the operating room. No one asked me who I was. No one even seemed to notice me. There were two surgical teams, one for her chest, one for her abdomen. They poured what seemed like gallons of blood into her, but it seemed to pour back out even faster. Her heart stopped twice as they desperately sought to locate and staunch the bleeding. Twice they got it going again. The third time they couldn't. Finally, they gave up.

I wandered back into the ER and ditched the scrubs. In the waiting room, there was Clint with all four children. He carried two-year-old Terry in his arms. The doctors had just finished telling him that Rhonda had died. He was teary and red-eyed, but more composed than I was. He hurried over to me. We put our arms around one another. "Were you with her, Dr. K.?" I nodded.

"You're a born-again Christian, Dr. K., right?" Again, I nodded, lying silently but shamelessly.

"Did she suffer?" I shook my head, still unable to trust my voice and lying shamelessly one more time.

"We'll be all right, Dr. K. The Lord will provide. She's in a better place now." I envied him his belief.

I phoned Steve at his lab. I was afraid he'd hear about the shooting on the radio and worry about me.

Beside, I had no car with me. I needed a ride back to the clinic.

Someone had managed to get hold of Fitz. He was flying back immediately. He had left a message for me to make sure the clinic remained closed the next day, Saturday. I also had a message from the police, requesting me to come down to the station to give a statement.

I was there for hours. I had to wait around while they questioned Mindy. Then it took several more hours for me to dictate my statement, wait for them to type it up, and sign it. The police only asked me a few questions about whether there was any history of animosity between Rhonda and Mindy.

Mindy was still there when I finished up. They had a few more questions to ask her. She acted lethargic, drugged. I guess she was still in some shock. She had been answering questions for a long time by now. I asked if she needed a ride home. She said yes. She had come in the squad car. We didn't say a single word during the ride.

The clinic was closed on Saturday and again on the day of Rhonda's funeral. Her whole church was there as well as everyone from the clinic, including Mindy. A number of her friends gave personal eulogies. As the last person to see her alive, I felt compelled to speak, and mumbled something about her sweetness, how we could be thankful that she didn't suffer, how she was probably smiling down on us from a much better place. I felt like such a hypocrite. I could barely stand myself.

Life went on. The clinic reopened. The University of New Mexico offered free counseling to anyone who wanted it. Clint, helpless in the real world, stopped by to see me several times over the next few weeks, asking for advice about bills and money. The hospital bill for $38,000 had him puzzled, since he thought it should have been so obvious to them that he had no money whatsoever. I went with him to the hospital business office to talk it over. The family income, it turned out, was so low that they qualified for some assistance program or other that took care of the hospital bills. He thanked me and said not to worry, that the church would take care of their other needs.

Mindy took a month off. Then came back to work briefly before quitting for good. It couldn't have been a comfortable place for her. I don't know about the others, but I didn't know how to behave around her anymore. I didn't feel any animosity that I could identify, but I also had trouble looking at her directly. I could barely make myself talk to her.

Dr. G. moved on too, taking a position in an emergency clinic in Los Angeles. Working graveyard at a less busy hospital gave him more time to study for *Jeopardy!*. Also being closer, he hoped he could try out more often.

Dr. C. left for California as well, where she met and married a blond and bronzed surfer. She now works out of her home for a large pet food company, and enjoys raising her surfer-to-be son.

Dr. B. headed east. He had finally accumulated enough money, in spite of his monthly child-support payments, to buy his own clinic, where he could accumulate as many AG charges as his clientele would take. He really was an Eastern boy after all.

Within six months, I was gone as well. Steve and I moved to Boston. I lost track of everyone for a few years.

Then one day, nearly six years later, I got a newspaper clipping in the mail from a friend in New Mexico. It was about Mindy. The headline said, *Lawman's Wife Follows His Footsteps.* According to the article, Mindy had helped her husband Frank study as he was making his way through the Albuquerque Police Department Academy several years previously. Frank's long-time aspiration had been fulfilled. Mindy herself had become interested in police work while they studied together. Now she had graduated from the Academy too. Their lives had turned out better than they could have expected.

The article was twice as long as the one I had previously saved, the one reporting Rhonda's shooting and death. I was suddenly very angry. Irrationally angry. It was an accident, yes? Accidents happen, don't they? Mindy and Rhonda were friends. No one felt worse than Mindy, did they? Mindy wouldn't have hurt Rhonda for the world.

I no longer feel vaguely uncomfortable around guns anymore. I justifiably hate them.

CHAPTER 18

Michael Kelley, Kelli Kelley, and the Law

The last time I saw Dr. Michael J. Kelley, he stopped by my house in Albuquerque to give me a bouquet of flowers, a lovely book of photographs of New Mexico, and a fond farewell. I was moving back to the East Coast. Steve had gotten a faculty position at Harvard. I felt terrible about leaving but was trying not to show it. Michael presented his gifts with an exaggerated flourish, bowed briefly, gave me a peck on the cheek, and headed back for his car without a word. He looked like he was about to weep too.

I'm looking at that book right now. The flyleaf is inscribed, "Please remember us and New Mexico, for we shall sorely miss you." It is signed Max, Kelli, and MJK. Max and Kelli were his dogs. Taped to the facing page are snapshots of the dogs frolicking around the yard or lying inside the house, along with Michael's leggy blond wife lounging in the living room of what he called his "Taos House."

There is no question about remembering them, Michael in particular. He was possibly the most intriguing person I've ever met. Wherever he is now, I hope he is all right. The odds are against it though.

Michael and Kelli swept into the clinic one day—if someone who is a slender five-foot-two carting a cuddly Cairn terrier under his arm could be said to sweep. A dapper black man in a tailored Italian suit, he could have been any age between forty and sixty. He offered his hand enthusiastically. "You must be Dr. K. So am I. Dr. K, that is. Dr. Michael J. Kelley. Please call me Michael. May I call you Veronika? I despise formality. Here's my card. My home number is at the bottom in case you ever need to reach me after hours. You went to Cornell vet school. I saw it in the phonebook. So did I—go to Cornell, I mean. As one Cornellian to another, you're going to be my veterinarian from now on. Let's get to work on Kelli. She's a geriatric case. Fifteen years old, recently menopausal. Can I say that about dogs or is that just a people term? She's been PU-PD for the past week. It's got me worried."

His card told me quite a bit about him. *Michael J. Kelley, M.D., Ph.D., Endocrinology, Thyroid Nuclear Medicine, Internal Medicine, Diplomate American Board of Internal Medicine and Endocrinology.* He practiced out of the University of New Mexico Hospital, he said, and also taught at the medical school. He'd recently moved to Albuquerque from Tucson and was desperate to find a good vet.

His dog told me quite a bit about him too. She was cloudy-eyed and ancient, but sweet as could be, well-trained, and exquisitely cared for—groomed so fastidiously that you'd have thought a professional had been preparing her for the dog show of her life.

You couldn't help but be impressed. I couldn't anyway. A busy, high-powered medical specialist had brought his own dog to the clinic instead of having the wife, the maid, or the personal assistant do it. It was indicative, though, of how much his dog meant to him. After all, he was the family member with the medical knowledge to make informed judgments and decisions about his dog's care and treatment. It was best if he were there in person. I was delighted to have him as a new client.

I set about doing my standard physical exam noticing from the corner of my eye that he was watching me very carefully. Why might she be suddenly drinking and urinating so much? That's what he had just told me in doctor talk. At her age, it could be a host of things. Most things it could be were not good. And menopausal? It was hard to believe she was still intact, not spayed in other words. Dogs were almost always spayed long before this. Even prized breeding bitches get spayed once their reproduction peak has passed, which would have been many years ago for Kelli. Spaying helps prevent later uterine problems. I found nothing obviously wrong with Kelli. That in itself was pretty amazing in a fifteen-year-old dog. She had quite obviously had a lifetime of outstanding care and attention.

"That was a very thorough physical," he flattered. "I'm impressed. I expected it, of course. You being a Cornellian and all, but I'm impressed anyway. So what can you tell me?"

I told him that his dog was in remarkably good condition for her age, but that we needed to start with some standard lab work if I were to figure out whether the increased drinking and urinating signalled a major problem. Also, if I could perhaps glance through her medical history, it might help me think about the case. Could he get me her recent medical records? I might be able to pick up something from her trends in her last few routine exams.

"I'm afraid you won't find much information there," he told me. "Kelli has had some bad luck with her veterinarians. Her last one was Dr. Martinelli in Tucson. Graduated from Davis. I tried not to hold that against him, though. Ha! Maybe you've heard of him? Had a Ph.D. as well as the D.V.M. Developed a new procedure for repairing GDVs. Brilliant man. Board certified in internal medicine and surgery. You may have heard him lecture at one of your national meetings? No. Anyway, he was wonderful. A close personal friend, not just Kelli's doctor. Used to use my Catalina house for weekends sometimes. Liked the ocean. Odd for someone living in Tucson, eh? Fortunately, he never had to do anything with Kelli except routine vaccinations and wellness checkups. Passed away unexpectedly last year just before we moved. I'm afraid his practice closed after that. Sorry. Records just not available. Before that we lived in New York. That was years ago, though. Kelli was a just a puppy."

Michael was a delightful client, but then most physicians are. They are medically knowledgable, of course, and it always helps that we speak the same language. More importantly, their knowledge combined with the fact that they have money makes them willing and able to pay for just about any necessary diagnostic tests. Nothing can be more frustrating to a veterinarian than not being allowed to do the one test that would pin down an animal's health problem for sure because of financial considerations. That's a frustration we learn to live with though. Not everyone is well-heeled. We understand that. But when we can do all the diagnostics, when the client can understand need for them and can afford it, the odds are much better that our treatment plan will be effective. Physicians are understanding about delays too. They know firsthand how emergencies and other unexpected events can often back patients up in the waiting room. I've never had a physician complain about having to wait to see me.

Even by physician standards though, Michael was a dream client. He doted on his terrier. Plus he was one of those people that brightened up your day every time you saw him. Made you feel better about yourself. Always smiling, upbeat, and alert. Ready with a funny story. I later discovered that he was a riveting conversationalist. But he was also pleasantly self-effacing. And knew when to listen. He listened intently, completely rapt by what you were saying.

Right away he told me straight off not to think about the cost of anything. Run any necessary tests. Just keep him informed about what was going on. Money was no object where Kelli's health was at stake. If there was a specialist somewhere in the country that might be useful for Kelli to see, that was also no problem. He'd fly her out there if necessary.

I saw him again a few days later when the lab results came back. He had brought a massive arrangement of spring flowers for the office staff this time and was regaling them with some story about his life growing up in New York City when I went out to greet him. Grandly gesticulating like a stage actor, he had the whole office, including the waiting clients, laughing and hanging on his words. "Can we hire you to provide waiting room entertainment?" I asked.

"Hey, that would be fun. Great, I'll do it. Wait, no. What would my patients do? Have to give it a pass. No rest for the weary. When I retire. Get back to me then. I think I'll have a dozen dogs then when I've got the time for them."

The lab work hadn't told me much unfortunately, but a new look at Kelli did. She had a huge swollen bruise where I had drawn blood from her jugular. Obviously she had some sort of coagulation disorder. A coagulation problem, added to the increased drinking and urinating made me pretty sure of the diagnosis. I told Michael that I suspected his dog might have Cushing Syndrome.

"Ah, hyperadrenocorticism. Now that I think about it, it makes perfect sense. I should have thought of that myself. If Kelli were human I would have guessed it immediately. I suppose you'll want to run a dexamethazone suppression test to confirm. It's probably more sensitive than the ACTH stim test in dogs too, right? Have you got a good endocrinologist to do the analyses? If not, maybe we could run it in our lab at the hospital."

It had slipped my mind for a moment that he his specialty was endocrinology. But this is why it is so delightful to have physician clients. He immediately knew which tests needed to be done. I didn't have to justify it. "I send my endocrinology samples to Dr. Rheinlander at Michigan State, " I told him. "He's the best there is. Germanic, a bit blunt at times, but absolutely first-rate. The people around him are first-rate too. He does all my endocrinology."

Michael also showed up in person for Kelli's suppression test, which involves taking several blood samples over an eight-hour period. I told him such devotion wasn't necessary. We would take good care of Kelli if he wanted to just drop her off.

"Don't think a thing about it, Veronika. Had all my appointments rebooked. Kelli sometimes gets nervous at the hospital if I can't be there. No offense, but those clinic kennels don't compare with the comfort level she has at home."

So each time I showed up to take blood, Michael and I would chat briefly about his life, or art, or travel, or skiing. He was fascinating on any topic. He had worked his way out of the New York City ghetto to be accepted at Columbia, and went on to Cornell Medical School. After many years running a busy New York endocrinology practice, he left for the more relaxed life in the Southwest because of some minor heart trouble. He missed the dog show circuit though. He had owned several national champion show dogs. Tucson had been all right, but he preferred the more alpine atmosphere of Albuquerque. He had also found a trainer here he particularly liked. He was thinking of getting back into the dog show world. Did I like opera? He did. He was intrigued to learn that a good friend of my mother's directed operas in Santa Fe each summer. We'll have to all go together next summer, he said. He was thinking of buying another house in Santa Fe just to take advantage of the summer opera season. Did I like art? He was particularly fond of Matisse and Picasso. His Taos house had several originals and numerous prints. I'd have to use the house whenever I wanted to ski Taos, he insisted. I wasn't to consider staying in a hotel. He and his wife rarely were there and even if they were, the house had plenty of extra room for guests. The housekeeper kept the house constantly ready for visitors. The refrigerator and wine cellar were always well-stocked. I'd offend him if I didn't make use of it.

I was feeling pretty good about things. I had a wonderfully fascinating new client and he seemed to want to be my personal friend. He was generous with the many toys his wealth allowed him to possess. Even better, I had probably impressed him with my incisive diagnosis of his dog's medical problem, a diagnosis that he had failed to make even though it happened to be in his own medical specialty.

I felt a little bit less good about things when Dr. Rheinlander phoned me a few days later to say that the suppression test had been normal. No Cushing Syndrome. There went my brilliant diagnosis. I was suddenly depressed. We chatted a bit about possible alternative diagnoses. It could be anything, I reminded him, she was a fifteen-year-old intact female. I had never even seen an intact fifteen-year-old female before. Had he?

"Intact! A fifteen year old *intact* female! I never heard of such a thing. Why didn't you tell me?"

"I did. It was on the records I..."

"You really *should* have told me. How am I supposed to help you without exact information? This changes everything." Listening was never one of Rheinlander's strengths. Neither was tact. In addition to endocrinology, his other specialty was making clinical veterinarians feel like morons. That was all right. I could take it. He was, as he would be the first to remind you, a brilliant endocrinologist. "I need to run some more tests. Call back tomorrow."

When I phoned the next day, he was very excited. "We do have a steroid-secreting tumor. It's estriol, a type of estrogen. You need to take a look at the ovary. Let me know what you find. I'll want to publish this."

This was mixed news. If it really was an ovarian tumor, secreting one of the minor estrogens, there was a good likelihood I could remove it, spay Kelli and she would be fine. I could think of many more dire possibilities though. Rheinlander was right. Before putting her through surgery, I should probably take a look at the tumor with ultrasound to make sure that the surgery had some chance of success.

Ultrasound was still a novel technique in veterinary practices in those days. The machines and their use were very expensive. Veterinary clinics, even ones as well-equipped as ours, didn't usually have their own machine or the technical staff to operate it. Fortunately, we had an arrangement with the University Hospital where Michael worked. We used their ultrasound facility after hours. "Of course, do the ultrasound," he said when I asked him about. "I'm sure I could arrange an inhouse discount, but that wouldn't be fair, would it? I should pay just like everyone else. The hospital has to make ends meet. I'm lucky enough to be able to afford it."

I half thought that he might meet me there with Kelli, but it turned out that he was going to be out of town that evening. He apologized profusely, hoped he wasn't imposing on me too much by not being there. It was simply unavoidable. A commitment he just couldn't break. So he dropped Kelli off at the clinic that afternoon with instructions to do anything that I felt was appropriate after seeing the ultrasound.

I ultrasounded her that night. As suspected, she did have an ovarian tumor—a huge one—the size of a golf ball. By the next morning when he arrived to see how things had gone, the surgery was done. The tumor had been large, but not invasive. Kelli had done well under anesthesia. She was now a spayed fifteen-year-old and was likely going to be fine. Michael was enormously grateful. A huge bouquet arrived for me at the hospital the next day. The day after that another arrived. Flowers arrived at my house too. I thought I might have to open a flower shop at this rate.

I saw Kelli several more times, but not as a patient. Michael brought her along with Max, his new Bichon Frise. He had been serious about getting back into the dog show world. Bichon Frises are popular show dogs that look like ten-pound white powder puffs if competently and consistently groomed, but look like ten-pound mop heads otherwise. They are playful and affectionate and make wonderful pets. But to show them requires a lot of maintenance by professional trainers and groomers plus daily attention from the owner. Michael obviously loved this sort of daily devotion. I wondered whether he might have put himself through school as a professional dog groomer. That's how good Max always looked when brought in for his puppy shots.

These visits gave us more chances to chat. I discovered that he had a sister who lived in Denmark. I love Denmark. Then we discovered that we both liked to visit Greece most out of all the countries of Europe. I liked the architecture best, he liked the sculpture. He suggested that the four of us, Steve and I plus his wife and himself, should vacation there sometime together. It would be his treat. What was the point of having money if you couldn't share the pleasure with your friends? He also let me know that he liked Swiss efficiency, but felt there was too much social pressure to conform there. Nevertheless, his five children were all in private school in Geneva where "the French influence softens the culture a bit." His wife complained about the cost, but she would see in the end it was worth it.

The only time I saw dogshow Michael rather than pet-owner or doctor Michael, he stopped by my house one Saturday in something of a panic. Gone were the sedately elegant tailored Italian suits, here was flamboyant Dr. Kelley. A full-length fox fur coat swirled around him as he stepped out of a pearl gray Mercedes convertible with a plumed hat that D'Artagnan and the other musketeers would have worn proudly. He worriedly handed Max to me. "Veronika, look at his eye. His right eye. What am I going to do? It's running. He's been blinking all morning. We're on our way to a puppy show. The judges will hate it. Can you do anything?"

"Michael, relax. This is nothing serious. Maybe a minor infection. Let me script you some antibiotic ointment. Stop by a pharmacy, put some in his eye immediately. Where's the show?"

"Santa Fe. I'm going to be late, I know it. Do you want to come with me? I could use the company. My wife was busy today. I should have phoned you last night. I'm sorry. We had friends over for dinner and it was past midnight before I noticed Max's eye. I didn't want to phone that late."

"Okay, in the future don't hesitate to phone. I've got plans for today. Maybe next time. Anyway, the eye may, or may not, be better by show time, but it's really nothing. In the worst case, Max will be fine for his next show."

Michael seemed grateful for my reassurance. I patted Kelli, who sat wagging her tail in the backseat, as Michael climbed back aboard the Mercedes and screeched off to the pharmacy.

Not long after that, Steve and I left for Boston. I continued to hear from Michael though. He was always an informative correspondent, and occasionally he would even phone for a bit of veterinary advice. He would tell me about Kelli's health, how Max was doing in the show world, where he and his wife had been travelling, the new art works he had purchased. He also continued to invite us out to his Taos house. By summer, he said, he would have a Santa Fe house too, and we could all go to the opera together. Perhaps my mom could introduce him to her friend, the opera director. He must be a remarkable person, growing up in a small town in the Adirondack Mountains yet going on to become a world famous opera director.

Just before Christmas, I received a sad letter telling me that Kelli had died. Fortunately, she had died in her sleep. No pain or suffering or lingering debility. He thanked me again for being such a wonderful doctor for her.

Then the letters stopped. I heard nothing for several months. Then letters started arriving from my other Albuquerque friends and these letters were *about* Dr. Michael J. Kelly. Newspaper clippings accompanied the letters. Michael Kelley was in jail, held in lieu of $500,000 bail. Michael J. Kelly wasn't his real name at all. In fact, no one seemed sure what his name was. He had been using at least seven aliases. His Mercedes was registered under the name of Josef Perregaux. He had written prescriptions for heart medication to a Gerald Thomas Lampkins. Using his variously aliases his age was fifty-one, or fifty-four, or fifty-six. Lampkins was probably his real name, police believed. If so, his origins were in Kansas City, Missouri, not New York City. He had an arrest record going back thirty years for crimes ranging from forgery to larceny to kidnapping. He had served time in the federal prison at Leavenworth as well as had stints in county and state prisons in Missouri and California.

I was having a hard time believing any of this. There must be some mistake. Police make mistakes all the time.

And yet, when I began to think back on it, some things that I'd never considered began to make more sense. He had almost always had the time to accompany his animals on veterinary visits. Given the schedules of most other doctors I know, that was remarkable, despite his devotion to his dogs. However, it wasn't so remarkable if he were just playing at being a doctor. I also remembered that when I had taken Kelli for her ultrasound to the University Hospital where he supposedly worked, he had been conveniently busy. His medical knowledge had always impressed me, but now it came to light that he had been a medical transcriber for years. That had given him the vocabulary, but he also picked up medical concepts and enough knowledge of physiology from his own study to understand much of what he transcribed. My hunch that he had been a professional dog groomer at one point in his life suddenly seemed a lot more likely.

I'd never actually met his wife either, although he had shown me numerous pictures of her. He apparently told other people that he was divorced or widowed or that his wife lived in Washington, D.C., or was a physics professor at Vassar College who had stayed in New York when he moved because her mother was ill. I'm curious now who the woman might be whose photo with him in the "Taos house" is in my New Mexico book.

Despite these revelations about him, I'm still inclined to give him a break. His love for his animals was certainly unfeigned. Also, no one ever accused him of trying to set up a false medical practice. Mostly he had given friends medical advice, or prescribed them medications, which were reasonable for the symptoms they described and safe in any case. He had also apparently prescribed himself heart medications under the name Gerald Lampkins. None of the prescriptions he wrote were for highly controlled substances, which might have substantial street value. They were mostly for antibiotics and ibuprofen. Was self-aggrandizement such a crime?

But the Bernalillo county officials didn't see it that way. They charged him with thirty-four counts, including fifteen felony counts for practicing medicine without a license and obtaining a prescription through fraudulent means. Eventually he pleaded guilty to four counts of making false statements on prescriptions. All other charges were dropped. He also admitted that he had previous convictions for forgery in California and Missouri, which qualified him as a repeat offender under New Mexico law. He was sentenced to eight years in the state prison near Santa Fe. Pretty hard time, it seemed to me, for some harmless prescriptions.

I felt terrible when I learned this. I kept thinking what a small, delicate, almost effeminate man he was. What joy he took in life. How that joy would certainly be crushed out of him now. The New Mexico State Penitentiary is one of the roughest in the country. In 1980, one of the countries worst prison riots had taken place there. Thirty-three inmates died, all at the hands of other inmates. Some had apparently been tortured, their bodies horribly mutilated. I had even visited the place myself, taking some pets there as part of a Humane Society Outreach program. After numerous instructions about what I could and couldn't do, what

I could and couldn't about talk to the inmates, I was locked in a cell for an hour with seventeen of the scariest looking men I'd ever seen. The inmates had qualified for this privilege with good behavior, and they were all very nice to me and the animals. But I was spooked. I turned down several subsequent invitations to repeat my visit.

I think I may have even been moved to protest this sentence in some active way, perhaps help him arrange appeal, except there were the lingering questions about where all his money had come from. Some came from an insurance settlement. Michael (I couldn't help think of him by that name) had already told me this story. He told it with tears in his eyes.

Ronnie was an underprivileged eighteen-year-old part-time restaurant cook, whom he had taken under his wing to try to help straighten out his life. He let Ronnie move into his apartment, rent-free. One thing he convinced Ronnie to do was to learn to save money. When he had saved enough, he asked Michael's permission to use the money to buy a motorcycle. Michael at first refused, but then relented when Ronnie told him he would buy it even without his permission. One early winter morning at breakfast, Ronnie made a point of telling Michael how much he loved him, thanked him for all the help he had been, and then rode off to work on his new motorcycle. That night, on his way home, Ronnie was killed in a traffic accident on a New York expressway.

In fact, as I later learned from the newspapers, these events did not happen in New York, but in Oakland, California. Ronnie collided with an oncoming car. The next day, Michael picked up the pieces of Ronnie's motorcycle and disposed of them. Intriguingly, just two weeks previously Michael and Ronnie had taken out $100,000 insurance policies on one another. When Allstate paid up six months later, with the double indemnity clause and interest, Michael received $203,365.

Investigators even at the time were speculating about the convenient timing of the accident, of course. But Michael's criminal past had not been uncovered then, and several years later when they considered reopening the case, no new evidence had surfaced that might implicate Michael in the accident. Allstate was not happy about the settlement though. Eventually they sued him for reimbursement of the settlement money plus $600,000 in punitive damages, contending that he had represented himself as Ronnie's stepfather when they applied for the insurance. It was a subpoena from this civil suit and newspaper coverage of it, which had blown Michael's cover and led to his arrest.

These events were worrisome in other ways. According to police records in Oakland, Michael was living in an opulent apartment even before the crash. Where had that money come from? Also, a wealthy couple in Albuquerque, who were his close friends, had told investigators that Michael had grown agitated one night when they told him their teenage daughter had been diagnosed with a learning disability. He angrily told them that the daughter's only problem was their liberal parenting techniques. He offered to let their daughter move in with him, so he could help her straighten out her life.

It does make you wonder.

But I'm still inclined to give Michael the benefit of the doubt. He was unremittingly kind to his animals. I've always thought that was a hallmark of a person's true character. Perhaps he outgrew his criminal past. Some people do. As smart and personable and energetic as he is, he could do well in the legitimate business world. I hope he survived his prison experience and became a stronger person for it. Maybe he is a free man again, still making those around him fell better about themselves. If I run into him one day at a dog show, I'll certainly remember that I owe him a peck on the cheek.

CHAPTER 19

Fortunately, I Have Just What You Need

Some key veterinary medical skills go unrecognized even by doctors themselves. Surgical and diagnostic expertise are easily appreciated, but few understand the subtleties that go into precise and proficient pet placement. Finding homes for animals that would otherwise be euthanized is a specialty that I didn't invent but I like to think I've perfected.

As evidence, consider that not long ago I was asked to help close down a research colony of seventy-six cats and I'm proud to say that I found homes for them all.

I also find myself on the Rolodex of every greyhound rescue club because of my particular talent.

It's not widely publicized, but when a greyhound's active racing career is over, it doesn't move into retirement home and live on a pension. It is either given away to someone who wants it for a pet or else it is euthanized. Given all the greyhound racing in this country, we are talking about hundreds to thousands of dogs per year. Clubs of greyhound lovers now exist for the sole purpose of finding homes for these dogs. Fortunately, greyhounds make wonderful pets. They are small dogs in the body of a large dog, affectionate, docile, just happy to be wanted.

They are also popular blood donors, so veterinarians like to have a few on hand if possible. Having been bred to run a mile at top speed, their blood is particularly rich in red blood cells. Consequently, it can carry a lot of oxygen, a helpful trait in transfused blood. As in people, blood types between canine donors and recipients have to match, so large veterinary hospitals need a number of different donors on hand to be sure they can match all blood types. I think our hospital has eighteen donor greyhounds at present. Our dogs used to live in the hospital kennels, but we now place them with private families, giving them free medical care for life, just so they can be brought in on short notice if blood is needed. I placed most of these animals too.

If you've ever tried to give away a litter of new kittens, you've probably noticed that it isn't all that easy. How, then, do I manage to find homes for scores of animals per year, usually adults rather than cutesy, cuddly newborns, often after they have undergone some major medical procedure?

You have to start with the proper mental attitude—the same attitude that successful salesmen have. You view each potential adopter as someone who will try to resist you, and your job is to find a way to break down that resistance, exploiting any and all weaknesses you can find. With the cat colony, for instance, I started with the freshman vet students. I had a few things in my favor right away. For one, I was an instructor and they were new students. They never could be quite sure what the consequences of refusing me might be. Then too, I could assume they were animal lovers. This would hopefully be true of most of them. Finally, I knew from remembering my student days that many of them would have assumed that pets would be unnecessary distractions from the overwhelming demands of their first year courses. This meant that many of them would have arrived at school one or more animals below their PPQ, personal pet quota. My job was to make sure that quota was achieved and maintained. The freshman students ended up with a lot of cats that year.

You also need to be constantly sizing up your friends, acquaintances, and colleagues to see how close each of them is to their PPQ. If it's a couple, you need to figure out which of the pair has the higher quota and work on that one. This is how I've been so successful with my colleagues Tom and Linda. They are both veterinarians. Tom is a pathologist, Linda does horse medicine. They live on a large farm, meaning they have lots of space for lots of animals. More importantly, they are exceptionally sweet people who hate to disappoint anyone. Now there is a feeling you can work with.

I've had to work on Linda particularly hard in recent years, because Tom hasn't been as receptive since I talked them into taking Tazzy, the three-legged Australian blue heeler. Tazzy was the first animal I placed with them. Not knowing how resistant they might be at the time, I left nothing to chance, used all my weapons. Tazzy was a hit-by-car stray. He was a bit snappy, so we named him after the cartoon character, Taz, the Tasmanian devil. It was pretty clear that his leg would have to come off. I knew there was little chance of anyone adopting an injured animal that would immediately need expensive surgery, so I went to Jim Lincoln, our orthopedic surgeon. "Tom and Linda said they would take the heeler if they didn't have to pay for the surgery," I fibbed. They hadn't exactly agreed yet.

I went to Tom and Linda, "Jim promised do the surgery for free if we only had someone to take him." This was almost true. He was thinking about it anyway. I wasn't finished with my pitch. "Of course, only professionals would be able to care for him properly. Jim would sure be disappointed to do the surgery then have to euthanize him later." I am shameless when I have to be.

But it all worked to perfection. It was a match made in heaven, except for the fact that Tazzy continued to be a bit snappy and not long after his adoption, he semi-accidentally bit off part of Tom's ear off during a disagreement over couch space. The Mike Tyson of blue heelers, it seems.

Given the ear issue though, when next I had a rescued greyhound to place, I thought I should approach just Linda and let her pass information along to Tom. Linda, I was pleased to discover, adores greyhounds. This was taking candy from a baby. Unfortunately, we learned later that this particular greyhound had a habit of eating eyeglasses. Okay, he didn't exactly eat them, but he would crunch them pretty much beyond recognition. Linda didn't wear glasses but Tom did. The first pair of glasses that Tom lost to the greyhound, he thought was probably due to carelessness on his part. Maybe he dropped them near the dog's food dish. The second pair he knew for sure had been on his desk though. Tom no longer looked so pleased to see me when we passed in the hospital corridor. The greyhound snatched the third pair off the top of a bookshelf where Tom assumed they were hidden. The greyhound had to have stood on its hind legs to reach them. Being the gentle and decent soul that he is, Tom now felt that he had no choice but to change not dogs but optometrists. He was too embarrassed to go back for a fourth new pair of glasses in such a short time. I tried to avoid encountering him in the halls. Through the grapevine I heard that the greyhound had become an outdoor dog.

Fortunately, I redeemed myself with Sherman, the pig. By now, Tom and Linda had more than a menagerie. It was more like a small petting zoo. They had indoor and outdoor cats, indoor and outdoor dogs, indoor and outdoor turtles, a few goats, a few horses. They needed a pig, I told Linda. She thought this would please Tom. He always had a soft spot for pigs.

I don't really remember where I got the pig, but I do remember that Tom and Shermie hit it off right away. When Tom was doing his evening chores, Shermie would snuffle after him faithfully. This pig only had one disconcerting habit. It was disconcerting to me anyway. Someone, maybe as a sick joke, had introduced him to SPAM, which is after all an acronym for SPiced hAM. Shermie became cannibalistically obsessed with eating SPAM. He would do anything, gymnastics, the hula, anything for a can of SPAM. Which was fortunate in a way, because he must have also been part bird. A couple of times per year, when nature beckoned and the migratory urge overcame him, Sherman would suddenly bolt and be gone for days. At first, Tom was desperate. Rural Idaho, where they live, is not necessarily a safe place for free-range edible animals. If the human hunters don't get you, the cougars very well might. Then Tom had a stroke of genius. He hopped into his pickup and cruised the countryside shaking that bright blue SPAM can out the window. Sherman could apparently spot that can from miles away. Soon a flurry of excited grunts would signal that Sherman was on his way in a headlong piggy sprint, making straight for the pickup. It was rather touching in a perverse sort of way.

Most people are not as easily convinced as Tom and Linda that this or that particular homeless animal is the answer to the gaping hole in their emotional life. Success depends on sizing up your victims carefully, and being as devious as you have to be. Estimating a person's PPQ is something of an art, but there are clues you can follow, such as how they respond to other people's pets encountered on the street, or whether they have recently lost a pet or are about to lose one. I'm not above moseying down the hospital corridor with one of my charges on a leash and "accidentally" running into a client whose pet is the same breed, but older, with a disease that will soon kill it. This allows me to help them in their later bereavement by mentioning, "Remember that cute Chihuahua, the same color as your Freddy (rest his soul), that you saw me walking in the hall last month? We fixed the problem with his heart, but I haven't been able to find a home for him yet. He's as good as new. I hope we don't have to put him to sleep after such a successful surgery." Sometimes I begin softening them up even before Freddy passes away.

I don't apologize for these tactics. The best cure for pet bereavement really is a new pet. And lots of animals do get put to sleep because they don't have homes. I'm just using my experience to perform one of those thankless public services, like garbage collection, that makes life on this planet more enjoyable for everyone.

With that bit of self-justification out of the way, I'll reveal another of my secrets. You almost never come straight out and ask someone to adopt an animal. It's a big decision with long-term implications. No, you ask them to take care of it for a just few days while it recovers from its surgery or sickness or something else you may have to invent. If you've chosen your prey wisely, a true animal lover will become too attached to an animal within a few days to relinquish it again, especially if its future, if not adopted, is uncertain. If a few days doesn't seem to have done the trick, I have ways of stretching things out a bit.

As long as you've chosen the right people, good people who appreciate pets and treat them well, these methods are pretty infallible. I have no doubt that many of my clients see right through my stratagems, but they work anyway because I'm only facilitating what the people really want. They just may not yet realize this is what they want. Or they may realize it, but not be willing to admit it to themselves yet.

One of my more masterful coups involved the Bosserts, Masters of Harvard's Lowell House. As one of twelve residence halls where Harvard undergraduates live, Lowell house, not surprisingly, reeks of rather stiff tradition. Portraits of the many Lowells who attended

Harvard beginning in the early 1700s peer from the walls of the dining room. Each year the residents celebrate the birthday of Abbott Lawrence Lowell, President of Harvard from 1909 to 1933. The Master's toast to President Lowell highlights the evening, tradition dictating that each year the toast must be in a different language.

The Bosserts, Bill and Mary Lee, loved the traditions but were anything but stiff. Bill, tall and dignified, with a silver-haired air of soft-spoken authority, looks like the central casting version of a Harvard professor. Mary Lee reminds me of an energetic and enthusiastic small bird. She is elegant and slight, maybe weighing ninety pounds after a massive feast. She loves to prepare massive feasts and organize the many social events the house has each year. They loved socializing with students and they had a calm and reassuring presence with which to face the variety of problems that even Harvard students encounter and create.

Steve and I became good friends with the Bosserts when Steve taught at Harvard. Steve was a member of the Lowell House Senior Common Room, and we saw them regularly at official functions.

The anomalous part of the Bosserts's lives was their pets. Having any sort of pet in this environment would be a challenge. What if your cat knocked over the cookies or your dog lifted his leg at Thursday High Tea?

However at the first formal party we attended at Lowell House, we noticed an elderly golden retriever, Abbott, meandering regally among the gowned and tuxedoed crowd, detouring around the *hors d'oeuvres* without giving them so much as a glance. Abbott belonged to the Bosserts.

Abbott affected a placid aloofness. Actually he craved affection and was hoping someone in the crowd might scratch his head. Having had a good Harvard upbringing, he knew better than to even think about disturbing the cheeses or caviar. Bill or Mary Lee walked him every day in Harvard Yard. They were as reliable a sighting there as the falling of the elm leaves in October or the statue of John Harvard.

They also had a house rabbit named Archimedes. Ark didn't usually appear for formal occasions. Like all rabbits, he had an insatiable urge to nibble and tended to nibble the house's curtains. After I let Bill and Mary Lee know that rabbits couldn't vomit, hence the curtain nibbling could lead to a serious intestinal blockage, they had all the curtains in the house shortened so that he couldn't reach them. What a wonderful couple.

As the years passed, each time I saw Mary Lee I would inquire about Abbott's health. He was getting on and I thought I might be able provide some useful medical advice. One day she phoned. Abbott was listless, not eating. I referred her to a friend of mine who operated an excellent animal clinic just across the river from Harvard. He kept me apprised of Abbott's gradual decline. I also began phoning some of my friends who were golden retriever breeders. Might they have an animal that needed a good home in the near future?

At the Winter Waltz that year, Mary Lee told me sadly that Abbott had had to be put down. Even the always upbeat Bosserts seemed sad. The Winter Waltz didn't have its usual *joie d'vivre*.

So when, a few days later, one of my breeder friends got back to me to say that she might have an animal available, I was elated. There was a problem though. Rusty had a badly fractured a leg, and despite just having had hugely expensive orthopedic surgery, he wasn't healing. His owners were broke, discouraged, and thinking seriously of having him put down, if my friend wouldn't take him.

Of course, she did take him. I soon discovered that the surgery on his leg had been performed by an idiot. I try not to criticize other doctors, but sometimes I come across incompetence so gross and damaging that I can't help myself. This was one of those times. I repaired the leg the right way this time at my cost, inserting a large steel plate to stabilize the fracture while it healed. Rusty would be fine. Then I phoned the Bosserts and invited them over to dinner.

By chance, Rusty happened to be recuperating at our house when they arrived. I told the Bosserts his sad story. They were appalled. If I could only find someone to take care of him for a few weeks while he recovered from the surgery. Steve and I worked long hours, so there was really no one at home during the day to make sure Rusty was all right, to give him his medications on a regular basis.

Back at Lowell House, Rusty fitted right in. There was never any question that he would stay. The students adored him and he adored them. Bill, an enthusiastic pilot, even had a mat and harness for Rusty installed between the seats of his airplane. He was no Abbott though. No strolling sedately among the *hors d'oeuvres* for him. Food of any sort was his primary passion in life. He once dragged Mary Lee halfway across Harvard Yard to pounce on a hotdog bun, which had dropped like manna out of the sky. He never saw the squirrel that dropped it, and after that he always bounced through the Yard on full alert, looking hopefully skyward. Mary Lee had to give up walking him after that, in fear that he might pull her off her feet and drag her around like a runaway stagecoach.

The last time I saw Rusty was after we had moved to Idaho. He and the Bosserts flew out from Boston in Bill's plane so that I could give him annual checkup. It was a delightful reunion. Rusty had grown a bit plump since I last saw him. He must not be over the food thing, I thought.

Actually he was over it though, Mary Lee told me as we sat down to dinner later on at my new house in the Idaho countryside. To teach him some manners around food, they had taken him to obedience school. A few weeks of professional training had done the trick. It was such a relief not to have to watch him every second. She was even walking him around the Yard again.

Cleaning up after they left that night, I couldn't find the brick of Brie. I knew we hadn't finished it. I never did find the brick of Brie. But I did find the plate it had been on, licked very clean.

CHAPTER 20

Kosrae

Picture this. A tropical isle with rugged, lush mountains, beaches strewn with seashells of every description, coconut palms bending into the breeze. This is Kosrae, the sleeping lady, two thousand miles from anywhere. I couldn't believe I was actually taking a vacation.

It was a vacation for me anyway. Steve had come on a mission to capture mice. That's right, mice. The same critters which, if given a half a chance, will ravage the pantry. These mice were to be shipped in regal mouse condominiums back to the mainland for his research on aging. I had come along as dive master and fun director.

Steve can get a little preoccupied with his work. Four years previously he had made another trip to Micronesia to catch mice. Micronesia is one of the finest scuba-diving destinations in the world with pristine reefs the equivalent of any in the world. Yet even though he is a rabid diver, he hadn't put so much as a toe in the water on that trip. I was along on this trip to inject a little perspective into his life. I've learned that all work and no play makes Jack—or this case, Steve—a pain in the rear to live with. Besides, I needed some decompression myself. My plan was simple. Lie in the sun, forget about the daily grind of work in the clinic, drag Steve away from his mouse-catching, and scuba dive as much as possible.

Scuba diving is something between a passion and an obsession for me. I find it simultaneously relaxing and exhilarating, like floating in outer space must be, but with more varied scenery. If I'd discovered diving earlier in life, I might have become a shark and starfish doctor instead. On my very first certification dive, I spied a large octopus wedged among the rocks. Of course, I dragged it out for a better look, and was thrilled to discover that it was huge—longer than I was. Its tentacles couldn't get a grip on my wetsuit, but it tried. I remembered what high school dating was like. That experience (the octopus, not the dating) probably hooked me on diving for life. Now I could hardly wait to slip into the clear tropical water to spy on the urchins and reef fishes and admire the fairyland sculptures of brilliantly colored corals.

We were booked at Kosrae Village in the sort of bamboo and thatch bungalow that defines one's image of a tropical idyll. It might have been straight off the set of *Swiss Family Robinson*, but with electricity, hot water, and a refrigerator to keep the drinks cold.

Of course, no matter where I am I notice the animals. Islands, particularly islands as small and isolated as Kosrae, are noted for harboring relatively few species. Without an airplane ticket, it's just too difficult to get there. So until humans arrived sometime within the last two thousand years, Kosrae had no snakes or leeches, no frogs, fleas, bees, ants, or worms. The lone mammal was a fruit bat. Only about twenty species of birds haunted the jungle, even if you counted the seabirds. Of the species that still existed, my favorite was a spectacular red and black honeyeater with a delicately decurved beak like a scimitar. On the other hand, to compensate for the few species, there are massively dense populations of the species that are there.

So for 99 percent of the island's history, animals of the sort we are used to—vultures, opossums, rats, dogs, cats, raccoons—were nonexistent. Their role had not gone wanting over the millennia though. Nature always finds a way. The dominant species here were crabs.

And crabs were of every sort and everywhere. Coconut crabs, mangrove crabs, hermit crabs, fiddler crabs, ghost crabs, shore crabs, sand crabs, soldier crabs. Crabs in the trees, crabs in the sand, crabs in the shower, and lingering by the commode. You wanted to turn on the light before stumbling around in the dark.

Sitting on the veranda sipping my morning coffee, I could see literally hundreds of crabs rustling among the palms without shifting my position. Sand crab burrows pockmarked the sand. They could be enormous—the size of a landmine and just about as dangerous. You had take care not to step in their burrow and twist an ankle. The burrow-owners always stood guard near the entrance, occasionally sallying forth to grasp something in their sturdy claws and drag it down into their homes. They would drag away anything that might fit—leaves, shoes, wristwatches, bottle caps, sandwich wrappers. One Village resident dropped his car keys and probably would have lost them forever if the piece of pink yarn he had attached to them hadn't turned out to be just a bit longer than the sand crab's burrow.

The prime scavengers were the hermit crabs. They seemed to outnumber the other species by hundreds to one. Steve caught more hermit crabs than mice in his traps by far, although whether it was due to their love of the peanut butter he used for bait, or just the constant random movement of thousands of crabs, we never were sure.

Hermit crabs, of course, have given up growing their own shells. They inhabit the abandoned shells of various snails. As they grow, they simply move into larger and larger shells. From the size of a peanut to the size of a pear, all seashells on the island seemed to be on the move. Although the beaches were virtually covered with shells, there still weren't enough for all the hermit crabs, and so they also stuffed themselves into plastic bottle tops, film canisters, or plumbing fittings when they could find them. It's one of the few places where your litter might come walking back into your hand.

As much fun as I had contemplating this wondrous abundance of crabs, I can never completely abandon my professional interests in dogs and cats.

Kosrae Village, for instance, had a stable of cats that showed up at the restaurant every night around dinner-time. Many of these cats were drop-offs. Knowing that the owners, American expatriates Katrina and Bruce, had a soft spot for cats, native islanders had begun dumping excess kittens at the Village. Two of these had just had kit-tens themselves. You could imagine a future in which the hordes of cats would swarm throughout the restaurant and begin to bother the more fastidious guests. My antennae twitch when I overhear anyone talking about animals, which they did one night at dinner. I heard Katrina tell someone, "I wish we could get some of these animals 'fixed.' Wouldn't you think we could advertise somewhere for a veterinarian willing to trade some free diving for a bit of minor cat surgery?"

This sounded almost like a proposition. Was there any way she could have known I was a vet? I leaned over and handed her one of my business cards. "Let's talk," I said.

Until I'd traveled quite a bit in the far reaches of the third world, I didn't appreciate that the concept of a pet seems to be a uniquely Western idea. The notion is pretty unthinkable in most places that you would keep an animal around without it providing you some economic benefits, and treat the creature with something like the same respect and affection you treat members of your family. The pet concept seems to be a luxury for those who don't have to worry about the source of their next meal. Elsewhere, animals tend to be seen as livestock at best, as insensate tools at worst—plows or tractors with legs. I've had to grit my teeth many times as I've witnessed friendly and otherwise kind people around the world casually treat their animals in ways that they would never consider cruel, but which would be condemned or even outlawed in the U.S. or Europe.

In Venezuela, for instance, I watched horses being broken, pretty literally. The cowboys, or *llaneros*, would first hobble all four of the horses' feet closely together for a few days so that they can barely walk without falling over. After their pasterns (that is, ankles) have been rendered sufficiently raw and bloody by the hobbles, they were blindfolded, saddled, and beaten by a rider until they have crashed into trees, fences, or to the ground often enough that they are too terrified and exhausted to resist anymore. Even after they are broken, Venezuelan cowboys would never think of giving them a pat or an apple. Why would you show any affection to a tractor or a plow?

I remember once trying to explain to one of these cowboys how we did it in the States. I told him that instead of having to chase down our horses every morning when we want to ride them like Venezuelans must do, we could just call them over to us like you would any other pet. He thought that was a pretty funny joke, and didn't believe me for a second. So I got more than a bit of secret satisfaction as I lay in bed in the each morning, listening to the *llaneros* yelling, charging about, and cursing as they tried to catch their horses.

So it was with the dogs and cats of Kosrae. The original settlers had brought pigs, canines, and chickens to provide a steady source of dietary protein. They brought rats too, and recent anthropological evidence suggests that even the rats were part of their diet rather than stowaways. I'm not sure about rats, but the other three species, including the dogs, are all still eaten enthusiastically today. Combine this practice with the Kosraen sense of ownership, which is pretty much that everything belongs to everybody, and some cultural clashes with tourists and expatriate residents are inevitable. One lawyer who was on the island to help codify the developing Kosrae legal system went home to England for a two week holiday and discovered upon returning that his pet Labrador had disappeared, no doubt into the cooking pot of one of his neighbors. Even one of the Kosraen dive masters, who had worked at the Village long enough to adopt the Western habit of keeping pets, came home one night to find that his older brother, in putting together a family feast, had cooked up all four of his pet dogs as part of the celebration. Dog surpluses on Kosrae will never be a problem.

As hard as these customs may be for me to witness, I don't feel I have the right to openly deplore the traditions of another culture. That doesn't mean that I don't deplore them, only that I try not to, and am quiet about it. After all, why we eat cows, pigs, and chickens and not horses, dogs, and cats seems pretty arbitrary when you think about it. In fact, we haven't always been so fastidious. I remember that the men on Lewis and Clark's exploration party were particularly partial to dog meat (which they purchased from Indians). They liked it better than elk, venison, or buffalo. I imagine that Seaman, Lewis's large black Newfoundland, must have spent many nights looking anxiously over his shoulder at the bubbling kettle.

If dogs are livestock to the Kosraens, cats are not. They are kept for another purpose though—rodent control. Rodents on the island can be a nuisance. Only the small, reasonably friendly, Polynesian roof rat arrived with the original settlers of Kosrae. But when whaling ships began visiting during the early the nineteenth century, they inadvertently brought along house mice as well as black and Norway rats, all species that live quite happily in the cracks and crevices of large ships or human houses. With few other mammals to compete against, these species thrived. So when cats finally arrived and began controlling the numbers of mice and rats, they were tolerated, if not welcomed, with half-open arms.

And cats unquestionably are efficient at controlling the smaller rodents at least. Steve never caught any mice in houses or stores that had cats. The problem with cats is that it takes relatively few of them to keep a rodent population in check, but that doesn't stop them from breeding. An excess of cats is as much a nuisance as an excess of rats if you don't like them. Thus Katrina considered it real progress when the islanders began dropping unwanted cats in front of the Village rather than simply drowning them or knocking them on the head with a rock. It would be nice to have the cat population under control though. I was hooked. So much for my pure vacation.

With luck, I might be able spay enough animals to make a difference. However, I might also be able to teach Katrina to neuter male cats on her own. What is that saying? "Castrate a woman's cat and you have a sterile cat. Teach her to castrate cats and she can amaze her friends, intimidate her enemies, and teach the tomcats of the world a little respect."

We had two problems to address right away. The first was the lack of any surgical supplies. There were no veterinarians on the island. There was a human hospital of sorts though. The hospital, in fact, could have used a few cats. Then they wouldn't have had to prop cinderblocks against the holes in the operating room walls to keep the rampant rats and mice from distracting the surgeon. So Katrina, as well-connected as you could be, called in a few favors and soon we were at the hospital rummaging through their supplies. They had a little anesthetic. Not my favorite type, but it would do. I hoped they weren't depleting supplies they might need for human surgery. They also had plenty of hypodermic syringes. That was good. Surgical gloves—a bonus. Lots of dissolvable suture, so no one would have to worry about removing stitches from the females. Perfect. What they didn't have was instruments. I could get by with just a scalpel blade if I had to, but a few other things would be useful. Katrina got back on the phone. The U.S. Army had a road building crew on the island. They had brought their own physician's assistant with them. He had some instruments I could borrow. We set up one of the Village's huts as an operating theater. By that I mean we cleared off a table in an empty bungalow with gaping a hole in the roof. A falling coconut tree had recently created the hole. But surgeons like lots of light, so the hole was in fact useful.

One problem was solved. I was ready to cut. Now I needed cats.

This was the harder problem. Even though these cats routinely strolled through the restaurant at night, and rummaged through the garbage at all hours, they were not real pets. They were feral. They lived outside, hunted outside, bred outside, occasionally died outside, and only survived outside as long as they did because they were tough, smart, and elusive. Someone was going to have to catch the cats.

Katrina had an ingenious idea. She managed to rummage up a bit of fishing net and fashion an impromptu cat trap. She spread the net in the open doorway of the main cat thoroughfare through the restaurant, tied string to the net's corners, ran the strings through a loop of rope which was slung over the transom and extended out to a table where she could sit, read a book, and be on the lookout for careless cats. A bit of raw tuna from the kitchen provided the bait. If any cats stepped on the net, she would yank on the rope hoisting them into the air. That was the theory anyway.

It worked pretty well for the kittens, which were naïve and a bit bumbling. I was soon at work. Of course, such a project attracted a lot of curiosity. Some of the workers repairing the hut's roof lingered to watch what I was doing until they saw me yank a testicle out of a scrotum. That usually sent them on their way again in a hurry. Also some of the expatriates on the island began to filter in, bringing their pets with them. Word travels fast on a small island.

Having anesthetized a number of animals now, I was pretty surprised at what I was finding when I examined them closely. First, even though these were outdoor cats they were virtually parasite free. The relatively few animal species that had made it to Kosrae apparently didn't include fleas, ticks, and mites. Second, I could feel a lot of healed fractures on their legs and paws. Some were even missing parts of their paws. What was this all about? Katrina reminded me how cats, particularly kittens, loved to bat things around with their front feet, and play footsie with small living objects. The crabs were easily the most available critters on the island to play this game with. Playing footsie with a grenade-sized crab in a hole is kind of like playing tag with hedge clippers—when you lose, you lose big time.

My favorite of these cats had lost big time. We called him Stumpy and he was a mess. Stumpy had only recently appeared at the Village. Half of one of Stumpy's feet had recently been amputated, probably by a defense-minded crab. It was healing well, though, as were a number of other scrapes, punctures, and abscesses. His fur was matted and ungroomed like he just didn't know how to take care of himself in the wild. And why should he? He had obviously been someone's real pet before being dropped at the Village. Although he tried hard to be wary and elusive, his heart wasn't in it. At the first encouragement, he would be rubbing against your leg, nudging your hand with his nose, jumping in your lap for extra attention. None of these endearing traits boded well for Stumpy's future, though. Not all restaurant goers appreciate them and restaurant owners have to pay attention to the wishes of their clientele.

In a day, I had "fixed" Stumpy, most of the kittens, as well as most of the real pets of the expatriate community. The rest of wild cats were posing a problem though. They were too fast or too strong or too smart to be caught in Katrina's trap. Come to think of it, this is probably why cats never caught on as a local delicacy. They were too much time and trouble to catch. I wasn't going to be on the island much longer, so drastic measures were called for. Katrina enlisted her hired help in the endeavor.

Although I'm certain this was not in their job description, they were delighted to be included in what was destined to become the local rodeo. Also, because Juspar was available, we decided to try a suicide mission.

Juspar was the night security guard at the Village. He was young, quick, and fearless—the sort of person who would dive into a cobra pit if you asked him and emerge with a grin, unscathed. Our plan was to entice the cats one at a time into the restaurant after it was officially closed for the night, corner them in a small area, throw a heavy towel over them, wrap them up in it and head for the surgery suite. The towel was necessary, of course, because frightened cats are no joke. With five weapons—four sets of claws and a mouthful of teeth—a cat is a walking armory. I also suspected some of these critters might be what we in the clinic call "exorcist" cats, able to whirl 360 degrees inside their skin in order slash, stab, and bite you.

I did my best to explain the plan to Juspar, but wasn't sure how much of my English he understood. At any rate his job, requiring his quickness and agility, was to stand in front of the open doorway and prevent cats escaping the restaurant once they were inside.

The plan was an utter failure but we succeeded anyway. We were far too slow to trap the cats in the corner much less throw a towel over them. They eluded us time after time. We and the cats were growing more and more desperate after each of our failed attempts. Finally, a burly tom bolted for the open door where Juspar, shirtless in the heat, belly flopped directly on top of it. I ran to his aid. He had somehow managed to grab its nape in one hand and front legs in the other. When he rose to his knees, I caught its thrashing hind legs which were dangerously close to performing on Juspar the surgery I wanted to perform on it. I wrapped it up in the towel and turned to see how bloodied Juspar was. He was grinning manically. This was great fun. Remarkably, he only had a couple of small scratches on his belly and one arm.

So this became our technique, relying on Juspar to body-slam and capture each cat. We had plenty of Clorox for his wounds and he seemed to enjoy it more than prowling the resort grounds in the dark. We managed to capture most of the cats we wanted this way, and amazingly Juspar avoided any life-threatening wounds.

There was one other cat I really wanted to neuter before I left. He had been described to me as a monstrous strutting male belonging to Peter and Kristen, a witty expatriate couple who lived on the other side of the island. He was the sort of pampered and well-fed cat that had grown so much larger than any of its feral competitors, it was easy for him to kick butt on the other males. He had probably sired most of the kittens in the area. If he were really as large as described, he would also be an excellent candidate for Katrina's first solo castration attempt. She wouldn't feel any obligation to be delicate with him.

Kristen was goofy over cats of any sort and so they had several. Peter, a lawyer in the role of long-suffering spouse, was willing to indulge her, though this one particular male (Mr. Macho, as I thought of him) was testing his limits. Mr. Macho was far too dignified to allow his owners to handle him, but as two highly educated humans, they were pretty confident they could outfox him with tuna and trap him inside a portable carrier. Their confidence was justified. Next morning I found him in his carrier in the "surgery suite" with a note attached.

Hi, my name is Kisrik. I am around two years old, and I love to beat up other cats. I also like to spray my owners' furniture, and sometimes my owners themselves. I have a very irritating yowl too. I was wondering if you could please remove my balls. I would really appreciate it. So would the other cats in my neighborhood. Thanks a lot.

Kisrik

P.S. I am quite tame, but I don't get handled all that often, probably because I am such an ugly, disagreeable beast. You might want to use heavy gloves if you try to pick me up.

Kisrik was as huge as advertised. His neck was too large for me to grip securely, so we gave his injection through the bars of his carrier. It took several times the usual dose of anesthesia to knock him out, but we finally managed it. Asleep on the table, he wasn't disagreeable at all. Katrina performed the surgery like an old pro and we left him in his carrier overnight, so that I could be sure he had recovered all right before returning him home in the morning.

In the morning though, the door of his carrier was wide open and he was gone. What had happened? We never found out. I suspect that one of the workers wanted to peak inside for a look at a larger cat than anyone on the island had ever seen before. He may have got a closer look than bargained for. Also, I couldn't guarantee that I hadn't left the carrier door ajar, since the previous day had included several dives and lots of spays. In either case, he was gone. So Katrina and I put our heads together to figure out how to break the news to Peter and Kristen.

As we batted ideas back and forth, it struck us both at the same instant—Stumpy! We went through the argument together. Kisrik is not really the kind of cat you want anyway. He sprayed, he yowled. What you two really need is a cuddly cat that needs you, one that you can pick up without risking your life. Stumpy is your boy. Sure, he looks a bit raggedy now, but Dr. K. examined all his wounds during surgery and they're all healing fine. Cats get along missing half of a foot with no problem. It will probably make him easier to keep in the house anyway. Just come over and meet him. Take him home on a trial basis. If you decide you don't want him, Katrina will take him back. I was up to my old tricks again.

And as usual, it worked. Seeing how pathetic and affectionate Stumpy was, it was love at first sight—at least for Kristen. They took him home in Kisrik's carrier.

As for Kisrik, he seemed to be making out all right. He was occasionally spotted around the grounds, chasing the other toms, apparently unaware that part of his anatomy had disappeared and that he was now supposed to be docile and contemplative.

I had really enjoyed my whole time on Kosrae, probably even more with the ad hoc spay-neuter clinic than if I'd really had a pure vacation consisting of nothing but diving every day and baking on the beach the rest of the time. If you were meant to do something, there is no greater joy than doing it. I was meant to care for animals. Sure the stress of the clinic might overwhelm me at times, but now I knew that I could get away from it all if needed, and still find a way to experience the rewards of helping animals and their owners. I'm already planning for my return to Kosrae. It really is a tourist's paradise. And there were still lots of cats on the island that were carrying around organs they would be better off without. Come to think of it, there are plenty of other islands with plenty of other cats that I'd like to visit too.

CHAPTER 21

Ike, the Irrepressible

Ike adopted me when he was four or five years old, a canny self-assured adult. I came home from vet school one day and there he sat in my favorite chair. He must have nosed the door open. He had also helped himself to some dog food from a bowl on the counter. He looked me over, apparently not too impressed. He looked over the two large dogs, Wart and Leo, that accompanied me. They didn't seem to impress him either. A very large, long-haired, gray cat, he blinked once, licked his lips, and went back to the nap from which we'd so rudely awakened him.

I was living in a house trailer in the country. In fact, I had moved into my trailer only the night before Ike adopted me, as if he had been waiting for an appropriate sucker to arrive.

I love Ithaca, New York, where Cornell is located. It's the quintessential picturesque college town. I'd lived in town my first year of vet school, but I've always preferred country life. A small inheritance that summer had been just enough for me to buy this one acre of land about fifteen miles outside Ithaca. The trailer was already in place. In order to begin my rustic living as soon as possible, Wart, Leo, and I had spent the previous month or so, while waiting for closing on the property, living out of a tent I'd pitched on the front lawn of a friend's house. As much as I liked my tent, the trailer was a pleasant step up in comfort.

My only close neighbors also lived in a house trailer. Our trailers were just within waving, or shouting, distance. Beyond them were large dairy farms. Directly behind both of us lay "my" woods. Technically, the six hundred or so acres of forest belonged to the local school district. However, because almost no one seemed to go into the woods, I developed a strong sense of ownership and got a bit prickly when the occasional deer or mushroom hunter strayed into them. The dogs and I soon roamed our woods every afternoon.

Ike, despite his self-satisfied nonchalance, was a mess. His long fur was matted and thatched with enough leaves and twigs that he resembled a small pile of forest floor litter with legs and eyes. He must have been living in the woods for quite some time. Before I groomed him into recognizable shape, I thought I should check to make sure he didn't belong to my neighbors, Fran and Boyd. After meeting them, I couldn't dismiss the possibility that they might own a cat that was gradually being overgrown by the forest. They might not even notice.

Fran and Boyd were wonderful neighbors, generous with their time and help, friendly in their own unique way. They were not, however, the sort of people I had grown up among. For instance, they hadn't even blinked the night I showed up at their darkened door, brandishing a large kitchen knife, wanting to introduce myself.

The day I moved into my trailer the big local news

was that three prisoners, all incarcerated for heinously violent crimes, had escaped from a prison not far away in the town of Elmira. So naturally that night when all the lights went out during a raging windstorm, I assumed the escapees had cut my wires in preparation for breaking down my door, torturing, and then murdering me. I grabbed my largest kitchen knife, crouched in a corner, and silently vowed to go down fighting. An uneventful half-hour later, I thought maybe I'd visit my new neighbors, just to help me feel a little safer. In case the diabolical escapees were lurking outside, I kept my kitchen knife with me.

Fran and Boyd's lights were out too, which was comforting. The windstorm had obviously blown down some wires somewhere. Unlike me, they had plenty of candles, lanterns, and flashlights. A wood stove warmed their trailer cozily. I eagerly accepted their invitation to sit down for a beer to get acquainted while we waited for the power to return.

When I say that Fran and Boyd were not like the people I had grown up among, I mean they were from a culture entirely foreign to me. I like to experience new cultures. It's one of the reasons I love so much to travel. Now I quickly learned, I could save the airfare and simply visit my neighbors. Fran, for instance, was a housekeeper at the local motel, whose favorite activities she told me were to fight in bars and give dancing lessons to her five-year-old daughter, Angela. Saying this with a chuckle, she instructed Angela to dance. Angela immediately broke into a sort of slithery bump-and-grind, which I previously had associated with places named The Xstasy Club or The Pink Pussycat. When finished, Angela gave herself a round of enthusiastic applause while Fran beamed proudly.

Boyd was a machinist at a local shotgun factory. He liked to haunt bars as much as his wife, but instead of fighting he preferred to listen quietly to country western music, and engage in extended discussions with his friends and relatives about world politics or who had gotten most drunk the previous Saturday. He also enjoyed watching Fran fight, he said, but he liked serious conversation better.

The two of them talked me into a friendly game of Uno while we visited in the candlelight. Uno is a card game in which the chief skill involves remembering to say the word "uno" when you have one card left in your hand. Boyd was very good at that, and I wasn't. Boyd knew that "uno" was a foreign word of some sort, and when I told him it was Spanish, he launched into a diatribe about all the Spanish-speaking people he didn't like. He particularly didn't like that Castro guy, who was in cahoots with those communists from Central America, L. Salvador and his brother Sam. All those communists could go take a flying leap for all he cared. I wasn't about to disagree with him, and since the lights came back on about then, I excused myself and returned to my trailer to process all the information I had gotten from (and about) my new neighbors.

Ike did not belong to Fran and Boyd. However, they had noticed him around for the past few months and had put food out for him occasionally. They had even named him

Ike, after one of Boyd's cousins who never washed his hair. So it looked like Ike was now mine, if he deigned to stay.

If he did however, I demanded that he look more like a cat. I brought home some sedatives to overcome his resistance, then did the only thing possible to return him to normalcy: I gave him the lion-cut. This is what we call a total body clip, removing all fur except the bit around the face. The twigs, leaves, and fur made an impressive pile on the floor. To make him look a little more like a real lion, leaving him a miniscule shred of dignity, I also left a tuft of fur on the end of his tail. Assuming that he would be living indoors most of the time now, his fur would grow back in and I could keep it groomed in the future.

Ike didn't seem to like his new look all that much, but since he was now getting a warm bed at night and all the food he could eat for free, he didn't complain excessively. The dogs didn't know what to make of this strange looking beast, which now looked kind of like a gray poodle only with sharper, faster claws. Ike had never been intimidated by them. Now they seemed to be the ones intimidated.

Some habits die hard. Ike remained a woods cat, never even thinking about hanging around the trailer during the day. Even though he didn't need the food, he continued to hunt. He never ate what he caught. Instead he presented his kill to me each day, neatly lining the corpses up in order of size on the front porch—bunnies then squirrels then mice, or perhaps pigeons next to sparrows next to shrews. I can't vouch for the flavor, but his presentation was delightful.

I often wondered about Ike's previous life. Had he

been living in the woods for weeks, months, or maybe years? Had he been abandoned on purpose? Or had he himself decided to abandon a sheltered suburban life and seek adventure in the wild world outside? Would he now be content with the sort of semi-domesticated life I offered, or was he a born vagabond? Whatever Ike's history, I soon realized that somehow he had become convinced that he was really a dog.

My late afternoon ritual was to arrive home from school and run Wart and Leo in the woods. Wart was my black Labrador, Leo was Steve's mutt. Steve was doing field research in Venezuela and wasn't due back for a few months.

Ike affected no feline aloofness. He always ran up from the woods to meet my car, then roamed with the dogs and me on our meanderings through the forest. I imagined that he even tried to mimic Leo's posture and gait. I began taking Ike on considerably longer hikes too. One time he climbed Ampersand Mountain in the Adirondacks with the dogs and me. I led him on a leash until his short legs got tired. Then I draped him across the top of my backpack, where he rode in stately grace like Indian royalty atop an elephant. When a hiker coming down the mountain informed me that I had a cat on top of my pack, I feigned surprise. "Must have dropped out of a tree," I quipped.

Ike helped me cut firewood too. It soon became apparent that I wouldn't be able to afford to heat my trailer with electricity during the long Ithaca winter, where it often stayed below zero for weeks at a time. I was scraping by on a few small scholarships and student loans. Trailers aren't designed to be heat efficient and my first month's heating bill—before it even got cold—was several hundred dollars. Fran and Boyd survived by cutting and splitting their own firewood. I had a woodstove too. It seemed the logical way to go. Boyd and I agreed to work together, cutting and hauling. Fran would provide moral support.

We had an agreement with the school district. We could take any fallen wood or dead snags in the forest for free. We weren't to touch living trees. Based on past experience Boyd figured we needed about ten cords apiece to make it through the winter. I did a little mental calculation. That was equivalent to a pile of wood four feet deep, eight feet long, and eighty feet high. I looked at the fallen limbs scattered on the forest floor, the few dead snags. "How much other wood do you have to buy?" I asked Boyd. He looked surprised.

"None," he told me, "there's plenty here."

I soon learned that Boyd had his own definition of "dead." Since it was late autumn, none of the trees had leaves. Boyd figured that any tree without leaves was a goner. "Too bad about that poplar," he'd say. "It'll never amount to anything." And with a quick shriek of the chainsaw, it would tumble to the ground.

So finding enough wood was not a problem. I did have some ethical issues to work through though. "Wait, Boyd," I'd occasionally shout in horror, "that's not a poplar, it's a wal...nut." Crash, the tree would hit the ground. Boyd had just destroyed several thousand dollars worth of fine grade cabinet lumber, not to mention a magnificent shade tree to save paying $80 for a cord of wood.

"No way," he'd assure me. "I've lived around these woods all my life. That's a popular." Later in the winter, he'd tell me that that was the slowest-burning, most aromatic, popular he'd ever cut.

Ike did what he could to help. The chainsaw didn't scare him. Nothing scared Ike. He wasn't foolhardy, but he could discriminate when situations were really dangerous and when they weren't. There were several dogs on the surrounding farms that unlike the bluffable Wart and Leo would have been bad news for Ike. He realized this and just avoided them. He'd been living by his wits for a long, long time. They weren't going to desert him now.

Ike would watch us cutting wood intently while sitting precisely where the next log needed to be stacked on our growing pile of logs. Then he'd trail behind us as we marched back and forth between forest and trailers, hauling the logs. He'd even watch us split it all. Hard physical labor was something he enjoyed watching. Besides, he was making sure we did it right.

When Steve got back from Venezuela in early spring, he immediately fell in love with Ike too. Just the two of them would hike in the woods several times a day when he took breaks from his writing. Although he was impressed by the amount of firewood I had laid away, and appreciative of Ike's assistance in the enterprise, he wasn't quite as thrilled as I hoped he might be to have Fran and Boyd for neighbors. For one thing, he didn't share Boyd's fascination with Uno. He was more a bridge and poker type. Uno was definitely not bridge or poker. For another, he didn't like the shiner I got when I made an ill-advised outing with the neighbors on a Friday night. Someone had thrown a punch at Fran while I sat next to her at the bar, chatting with her cousin. Fran ducked. I was looking the other way and didn't. We decided that our socializing with them should be confined to home. Then there was the issue of the birdfeeder.

Steve put up a birdfeeder as soon as the ground had thawed. It was a delicate business, locating it where Ike couldn't ambush its users. We finally put it about fifty feet from our kitchen window in the middle of our small lawn. Ike could be seen approaching from many yards away. The only birds in danger would be the exceedingly stupid ones. We kept binoculars on the drainboard to look for unusual species.

The feeder got Boyd's attention. Once after a lunch together, Steve explained to him about strategically locating the feeder so that Ike couldn't ambush the birds. He also showed him how to use the binoculars and taught him how to identify the three or four species that were feeding right then. He also explained a little about bird behavior, showing Boyd how to recognize which species were dominant and thus got first access to the seed.

The next thing we knew, Boyd had put up his own feeder, also strategically placed to minimize Ike's depredations. Steve was pleased that he had awakened in Boyd an interest in birds and their behavior. He felt a little more forgiving about the nights of Uno and my shiner.

Until one day when the unexpected sound of nearby

gunshots brought us to our feet. Looking out the window, we saw a few feathers floating from Boyd's feeder to the ground where several inert bodies lay. Steve ran toward Boyd's house, "Stop! Boyd! What are you doing?"

"Did you see those big black ones?" Boyd asked.

"Of course. Those are rusty blackbirds, remember?"

"They wouldn't let the little guys eat. Them black ones can't use my feeder."

Steve walked away, shaking his head. Ike later lined up the blackbird corpses on our porch.

Several years later, we moved to New Mexico. Steve had preceded me by several months, so I drove alone with all the animals. Ike sat the passenger seat, the back seat belonged to the dogs. Ike never seemed to lose interest in the passing scenery. He was probably wondering, as I often did, what it would be like to explore some of the places we drove through so quickly. At rest areas, I would put the dogs on leashes and let Ike out the door to follow us to the appropriate bit of lawn on which to relieve himself. People would often ask me in a slightly disapproving tone if I didn't feel nervous, not having Ike on a leash with all the people and cars and dogs around. "Not at all," I'd reply opening the car door so he could jump back into his seat, "Ike can take care of himself."

Ike wasn't all that thrilled with Albuquerque at first. We lived in the suburbs, so there was relatively little adventure to be had by his standards. However, when we moved to the nearby mountains a year later, he was back in his element. The pinyon pines and junipers were excellent places for ambushing bunnies, birds, and squirrels. Adventures lurked behind every bush.

One day Ike didn't sprint from the woods to greet me when I returned home from work. He still hadn't shown up by the next morning. This was not a good sign. Ike didn't miss meals.

I phoned the police, the Humane Society, and the closest veterinary clinics, asking them to let me know if a gray cat turned up lost or injured. I made "Lost Cat" posters, distributed them to all my neighbors, put them up in the local stores and restaurants, nailed them to all the telephone poles in the area. No luck. Several weeks later, while scouting the woods with the dogs, I found a clump of bones and long gray fur. An owl, a coyote, or a cougar had apparently done Ike in. I took down my posters, quit pestering the police and the Humane Society.

I was sad, of course. I grieved a bit longer than I normally do when a pet dies. Ike was such a character. But he did love his adventures. They made him the character he was. Adventures wouldn't be adventures without a bit of danger. His luck had just finally run out.

Several months passed in which I seemed to be busier than ever. In addition to my normal job, I volunteered my time one evening per week to spay and neuter newly adopted animals for the Humane Society. Although they have to euthanize a lot of animals, they just don't have the space to keep them indefinitely; they are in the business of saving as many animals as possible by finding homes for them. It was a worthy cause, which I wanted to support in a way that I could be of most help. Since I had been working with them, they had been allowing me to use animals that were about to be euthanized as blood donors, when I had patients that needed transfusions. The official understanding was that I would euthanize the donors after I had used them. But the mutual implicit understanding was that if I could find a home for the blood donor, I would quietly do it.

One Sunday afternoon, a hit-by-car cat needed an urgent transfusion. I phoned the Humane Society and asked if they had a large donor cat. I needed a lot of blood. Charlene, my contact at the Humane Society, told me that they had just the cat I needed. He was supposed to have been euthanized the previous night. His time was up. "But he's such a cool cat, I couldn't do it," she said. "Take him."

I sent my tech over to pick up the donor while I attended to the hit-by-car. When finally I was ready for the transfusion, I walked into the kennel to retrieve the donor and there was Ike. He was skinny, fur matted with twigs and leaves. He gave the loudest and happiest meow I ever heard when he saw me. I burst into tears.

"If you thought the last lion-cut was an indignity," I sniffled, "wait until you see this one."

I never did figure out what had happened to Ike. He wasn't about to spill the beans. I learned that he had been picked up in a wild shrubby area along the Rio Grande River. The spot he was captured was at least thirty miles from my house, on the opposite side of the city. My best guess is that he hopped through an open window of a parked car for a quick snooze. Maybe the car belonged to some hikers. Maybe when they discovered him, they had no idea when or where he had got into their car. Maybe they abandoned him along the river because they thought he looked like he could take care of himself. Or maybe it was a real Ike-like adventure. Maybe he had been abducted by a gang of drug-smugglers and had fought his way to freedom near the Rio Grande. I really didn't care. I had Ike back.

The other big surprise of the week was a phone call from Fran. We had kept in touch, barely. I sent them a Christmas card each year with a short note about what we were doing. I never heard back from them so I wasn't entirely sure they were still at the same address.

"We're not at the same address," Fran gleefully informed me, "we're in Albuquerque. How can we find your house?"

Fortunately, Steve was still aglow with joy at the reappearance of Ike. Otherwise I don't think he would have been able to face the fact that Fran, Boyd, and the kids (they now had a young boy too), people he had thought were safely in the past, were coming for a visit.

It was worse than a visit. They showed up towing everything they owned in a homemade travel trailer. They needed a place to stay while Boyd looked for work. Boyd proudly showed me his missing index finger. He had cut it off somehow in an accident at the gun factory. The settlement he had received was just enough to buy the travel trailer and keep them clothed and fed for a few months. He had heard, I guess, that opportunities abounded in New Mexico for nine-fingered shotgun machinists.

Steve put on a brave face. He did his best to play the

convivial host. Fran and Boyd had, after all, been enormously helpful to me when I lived alone while he was in South America. We thought the best treat we might offer visitors from the east would be a meal at our favorite restaurant—*The Rio Grande Cantina*. New Mexican food is like no other Mexican cuisine, Steve told them. He'd grown up in Southern California where people thought they knew what good Mexican food was. But New Mexicans had invented the most flavorful of all southwestern cuisine. Wait until they tried it, he enthused.

"You're right," Boyd informed him. "We know already. We stopped at the Taco Bell downtown for lunch." Steve and Boyd were still not on the same page.

Boyd never found a job in New Mexico. After a couple of weeks, they headed back to New York and we lost touch for good.

After his latest adventure, Ike seemed content to hunt closer to home than before. He came in earlier in the evening, left on his daily prowls later in the morning. Maybe he had had his fill of adventure.

When we moved to Boston about a year later. Steve went first again, I followed again with the animals. We now had five dogs and a parrot. They were all confined to the backseat. Ike, now getting along in years, still demanded the comfort and privacy of the passenger seat.

We moved into a sort of a country home on Boston's South Shore. We had an acre of land, and all our neighbors had about the same. This was the country by Boston standards. The neighborhood was tree-covered and shrub-strewn. There were plenty of birds and squirrels. It was just the sort of place that Ike in earlier years would have found irresistible. He still did roam, but he was no longer the hunter of old. He had lost a step or two. I thought cataracts might be clouding his vision a bit. Most of the animals he now presented me were moles or house mice.

I think he was probably going after a house mouse when he mistakenly bit into a 220-volt appliance power-line in our basement. The powerline drooped just slightly from the ceiling rafters. He would have had to lunge from the top of a nearby refrigerator to reach it. For whatever reason, he did lunge, he did bite into the powerline, it did electrocute him, he did fall unconscious seven feet on to the concrete basement floor.

Steve, meandering downstairs to call the dogs for dinner, saw Wart hunched over Ike, apparently eating him. Shouting "Nooooo," and charging down the rest of the stairs, he flung Wart across the basement. Wart yelped in confusion. Hearing this, I ran down from the kitchen. Surely Ike, the Indestructible, could not have been killed by an overly friendly, eager-to-please black Labrador.

Ike was still alive, but semi-conscious. He was so covered with saliva, he looked like a newborn goat still covered with afterbirth. Wart hadn't been trying to eat him, he had been licking him. Maybe thinking that if he licked Ike enough, he would come back to life. It seemingly worked. As I hauled him upstairs for a look in better light, Ike's eyes opened. He was completely limp and looking very confused. I noticed that Ike had what we call cord-burn. The corners of his mouth and tongue were charred black. I could now imagine what happened. Later we found the marks on the powerline where he had bitten it.

Most cats die when they bite into a 110-volt cord. Ike had survived a 220-volt bite, a long fall to a hard floor, and a tongue-mauling from a worried Labrador. I rushed him to the hospital, treated him with steroids and Lasix for the pulmonary edema that often kills electrocuted cats, and cleaned him up the best I could. By the time I was finished, Ike was pretty alert. Not his old self yet, but on the way. He even protested weakly when I carried him back to the car rather than let him walk.

He laid around the house for a couple of days, then returned to *his* yard once again, prowling for the unwary house mouse that might stray into his territory.

Ike's luck did eventually run out. In retrospect, it was probably for the best. He was not the sort of cat you'd want to see waste away into senility.

It was probably a year after Ike's electrifying experience that my wonderful Aunt Millie died unexpectedly. Among the things she left behind besides warm memories was Joel, her dog with the prosthetic eye that I had implanted years before after my dog, Leo, bit through the original one. Joel had a history eerily similar to Ike's. He had lived many years as a feral dog in the woods before opting for human adoption. For years after he had a cushy domestic life with Millie, he would still prowl the forest by himself, raising havoc with the local rabbits and squirrels. However, like Ike, he was pretty creaky and doddering now.

Naturally there was no question about where Joel would go. I wasn't too worried about him and Leo doing serious battle anymore. They were both past the testosterone frenzy of their youth. Joel spent most of his time lying around the yard. So did Leo. So did Ike. That was the problem. One day, Steve looked out the window of his study and saw Joel shaking a rag furiously. Then he realized it wasn't a rag at all, it was Ike. Ike must have been asleep when Joel snuck up and grabbed him.

He raced outside and beat on Joel until he let go. Ike was still alive, but barely. He raced Ike to the clinic, ran past reception and into the operating room where I was doing some minor surgery. Ike gave a few last feeble breaths and expired on my operating table before I could so much as check him over thoroughly.

We buried Ike that night in the backyard close to the place we would later bury Joel. Steve and I sat outside on the back porch late into the night, reminding each other of our favorite Ike stories. What a life, we decided. It was as full as a life could be. If Ike could talk to us now, we decided he would urge us to cheer up. He had no regrets. He had always lived on his own terms. He'd had nearly every adventure a cat could ever expect to have. "If he could talk to us now, maybe he'd finally tell us where he had been all those months when he went missing in Albuquerque," Steve laughed.

"And let us in on how he got there," I added.

The fireflies were blinking on and off over Ike's grave. I wanted to think they were saying good-bye. Ah, Ike, the Irrepressible. I'm sure there must be another cat out there with your noble spirit and flair for the dramatic. If there is, I'll eventually find him—because I'll never stop searching.

About the Authors

J. Veronika Kiklevich practices and teaches veterinary medicine at Washington State University Veterinary Hospital. After graduating from Cornell College of Veterinary Medicine, she worked in private practices in Albuquerque, New Mexico, and suburban Boston, before moving to her current position. She also has hosted radio and television programs of veterinary advice.

Her husband, Steven N. Austad, teaches zoology, animal behavior, and the biology of aging at the University of Idaho. He also writes and lectures widely to the lay public about science.

They live with their two daughters, Molly and Marika, and a houseful of pets in the mountains near Moscow, Idaho.